Table of Contents

Introduction

More than sixty years after the early miserable events that shaped the remainder of my life, I have now finally found time to write about them. In the intervening years between childhood and old age, memories naturally fade, in particular exact dates and times, but always certain stark incidents remain firmly implanted and are more readily brought to mind. It is peculiar how the worst memories always seem to last longer and can be retrieved more easily.

Many times, after having repeated to friends and family members certain factual events that occurred during my own childhood, spent in a Methodist Orphanage for over nine years between 1936 and 1945, the reaction to my narration was, "You should write about that!" My mother repeatedly suggested that my individual experiences and those of my younger brother and older sisters, who shared the same early existence, should be recorded. Unfortunately having never managed to write this particular book during her lifetime, it is now dedicated to her memory.

In the past there have been numerous stories of "Orphans" and Orphanages, both factual and fictional, relating to the treatment interns received in both state and privately run institutions in many parts of the world, particularly following major conflicts in places like Germany, Bosnia, and the former Soviet Union. Even today in Eastern Europe, the Middle East and Africa, children are still shown to be suffering in similar situations under the most appalling conditions, barely surviving. Naturally public opinion is shocked and reacts appropriately with necessary assistance.

New international laws have finally been introduced to reform a system that has, in fact, prevailed almost unnoticed for hundreds of years. More resources and regulations however are still needed to confront the problems of children in care, who are continually being subjected to numerous abuses which should have been eliminated generations ago.

A current American television news program recently described the fate of thousands of young children from fatherless families, or bombed out and broken homes in supposedly civilized old England, who, even before during and after the Second World War, under the cloak of "evacuation," were allegedly condemned to terrible hardships between 1930 and the late 1960s. It was disclosed that ships secretly transported these children, with British Government approval, to both Australia and Canada where the majority were placed in institutions and orphanages staffed by various religious groups.

The main reason, hidden for years apparently, was specifically to increase the population of Caucasian or Anglo Saxon immigrants in those "Outposts of the Empire." With the result that, even today as seniors, many survivors are neither a citizen of their birth country or indeed of any country, including Australia, because of bureaucratic bungling. It is incredulously shocking to realize that a British Government, who for years was so outspoken against the deportation of wartime refugees, allegedly secretly condoned such a program. A more recent, February 2010, newscast on BBC America showed Gordon Brown, the British Prime Minister, after decades of denials, finally publically apologize for the wartime governments "despicable decision". A large number of elderly expatriates were invited back to London for the apology where they described their own physical and mental abuses in Australian religious institutions, which were designated as "homes" in the 1940s "Child Migrant Program".

Not all "Orphans," however, were sent to Australia or Canada. To a lesser degree, hundreds of children from infants to teenagers were also being placed in homes and institutions run by religious groups in England, under the guise of "evacuation." A number were staffed by members of the Methodist Church. One of these "homes" was the Princess Alice Orphanage, the only one designated as an "Orphanage," named after Queen Victoria's daughter, who nursed her own children while afflicted with diphtheria, before dying early at the age of 37 on 14th December 1878. The following year, in 1879, a grant of ten thousand pounds was donated by a local wealthy industrialist, Solomon Jevons, to purchase ninety acres of land near the town of Sutton Coldfield in Warwickshire. When work finally commenced in 1882, the Wesleyan Conference contributed additional funds for that particular project.

In 1869, Dr. Thomas Bowman Stephenson, a Methodist minister, together with two friends, started the charitable organization known as the "National Children's Homes" in Lambeth, London. At that time, more than thirty years after the novelist Charles Dickens had exposed the exploitation of poor children in "Oliver Twist," there were still thousands of ragged urchins living wild in London and many other cities throughout the United Kingdom. Dr. Stephenson directed the growth of the National body for the rest of his life, establishing homes across the entire country. The Princess Alice Orphanage eventually became a branch of the N.C.H. which was headquartered in Highbury, London, where it remains to this day, now known as "Action for Children".

A recent letter in an English newspaper, sent by a retired gentleman, described his own early years in one of these homes. He wrote how all boys in the house were regularly beaten with a rubber shoe or cane and forcibly held under ice cold showers for minor infringements, such as refusing to eat the frequently inedible food or talking out of turn. There were instances when bed-wetting culprits were ordered to run around outside with a soiled sheet tied around their necks, regardless of onlookers, rain, heat or freeze.

Obviously during the war many children were made parentless and homeless, so there was a desperate need for such places. However, in the light of recent disclosures, doubt has been cast on whether all the children were indeed evacuated to those places abroad, with the certain knowledge or consent of any surviving family members. Many children, reportedly, never knew their parents or where they were born. There is also, allegedly, evidence that some surviving parents and siblings were deliberately misinformed as to the exact whereabouts of certain young children.

Conditions in English institutions were not, apparently so far reported, quite as horrific as those allegedly experienced by the inmates of Orphanages in Australia, who were reputedly forced into hard labor on building construction sites, suffering severe physical and sexual abuses by others in the process. Nonetheless, in Methodist controlled homes, the treatment experienced by certain individuals was also, at times, extremely cruel to the point of sadism. Considering the children were supposedly sheltered and fostered by such a prominent religious group, sanctioned by a government department, there should have been closer supervision to avoid or prevent the numerous instances of child abuse that occurred. Particularly when the individuals who administered corporal punishment, represented a church purporting to practice tolerance and forgiveness, as described in the stated principles of the Methodist doctrine. Even in wartime with so many restrictions and pressures affecting everyone, there was no excuse for such treatment of the young and innocent.

With few exceptions I have tried from memory to pinpoint the approximate time of individual incidents that occurred, particularly those coinciding with certain circumstances during the war. However, although dates and times may be approximate because of memory loss over the intervening years, the events and persons involved are indeed factual and forever engraved in my memory.

Not all experiences were unpleasant, although each one left an everlasting impression, with physical and mental scars still carried seventy years later. Unfortunately, multiple confrontations caused me to form harsh personal opinions that to this day are still held regarding this particular religion and those who expound it. Most certainly this was not the original intention of the ministers or sisters at the Methodist Children's Home.

With the exception of the first two chapters, most of the events described throughout the book occurred during the war between the ages of seven and thirteen. Chapter six, "The War", specifically relates to individual circumstances that not only directly affected the normal everyday routine, but also created a fearful anticipation and excitement that somehow made our usually humdrum existence actually more bearable.

Most of the related abuses happened to me personally, but obviously there were numerous similar situations involving friends and relatives. In spite of witnessing many, or being told of others, not all are recounted because I believe the narration should be a privilege of those persons who suffered them.

Reflecting on those early times, there is no regret, neither do I place sole blame on any particular individual, it was the way it was! However, it is my belief that no child, regardless of how poor or how underprivileged they may have been, should have suffered such harsh treatment through no fault of their own, particularly in a religious institution.

John Anthony Davies.

1

The Separation

In 1936 Adolf Hitler's Nazi troops invaded the Rhineland between Germany and France, prompting the systematic rampage of Europe and eventually World War Two. That same year my Father died after collapsing on August 16th from a debilitating heart disease following Rheumatic Fever, which was quite a common illness in the damp smog-ridden towns close to London. At the time of his death I was only four years of age and my brother Maurice was nearly three. We had four older sisters, the youngest Pauline, had just celebrated her sixth birthday the previous July. Audrey, Joan and Yvonne were consecutively between the ages of seven and ten.

Memories of my father are vague, except what my eldest sister Yvonne and my Mother related to me later in life. However, one memory constantly in my mind involved the smell of new leather and petrol, combined with the sensation of riding in a large open-topped motorcar, travelling along a country road on a warm sunny day. Only a shadowy vision remains of the driver wearing a dark suit and a black shiny peaked hat, apparently always my Dad.

Yvonne, who filled me in on many questions, informed me that in the early days, he was a chauffeur for a car hire company, who rented out "Posh" cars, such as Daimlers and Rolls Royce's, used for weddings and driving certain well known local dignitaries to meetings. Later he became the personal chauffeur for the Lord Mayor of Ilford, an Essex county town now a suburb of Greater London. Whenever possible my Father took me along on trips sitting next to him on the long, leather covered, bench- type front seat. On a full day off he would often drive the whole family to the coast, usually to either the nearby town of Southend-On-Sea or Westcliffe, two popular coastal resorts frequented by Londoners. On those occasions I was again privileged to be allowed to sit up front.

On one family visit to the seaside just before my father died, I apparently nearly drowned after being carried out to sea. The story was often recounted about what happened on one particular day in July of 1936. Dad drove the family to the coast and then left to fulfill a driving engagement, planning to return later to take us back home. Everyone was enjoying the beautiful day picnicking on the beach or paddling, while Mum was busily preoccupied preparing sandwiches and at the same time watching my younger brother, sheltering from the sun under a large brimmed hat. The rest of the family were playing in the sand or paddling in the shallows, while I floated on my newly acquired rubber ring near the edge. Somehow in the excitement of play, unobserved by anyone I slowly drifted out of my depth from the shore. Suddenly realizing her eldest son was no longer in sight Mum leaped frantically to her feet, running along the water's edge, searching and screaming my name. My eldest sisters hurriedly joined her after a brief few moments, which must have seemed endless, eventually spotting me floating away heading directly out to sea, close to the center of the old wooden pier. Two men fishing from the top of the pier heard the cries and dove off the dilapidated structure, swimming towards my gaily-bobbing figure, finally managing between them to drag me back to the safety of the shore. Quite easily my lone figure could have gone un-noticed and drifted beyond the end of the pier, where strong currents and the outgoing tide at the time could have borne me far out to sea, meaning this story may never have been told.

At the time of this incident the family lived in one of a typical row of dull, pebble-dashed semi-detached houses, in the lower income area of Romford, a small Essex county market town that also boasted a large Gasworks and Brewery. The obnoxious odors from both factories always permeated and clouded the surrounding air, where most employees of both companies lived in similar houses close by. Between the two factories at the rear of our house stood a large, oval-shaped, fenced in greyhound racing track, encircled by a high, metal-roofed spectator pavilion. Every Wednesday and Saturday evening the whole complex was lit by brilliant flood lights and the throaty roar of the crowds could be heard at the start of every race. Many patrons frequented the Kings Head public house situated on the opposite side of London Road, obviously attempting to work up enthusiasm before the races or bemoan their losses afterwards. Certainly many hard working men squandered their meager wage packets betting on the unfortunate greyhounds, or downing numerous pints of ale whilst commiserating their unaffordable losses.

Mum took in sewing for a living even while my Father was still alive, augmenting the meager income of that era by making most of her children's clothes. Residents from the whole neighborhood frequently knocked on the door with used garments to be altered, taken up or down, let in or out. Wealthier local residents often brought over patterns or pictures of clothes from magazines they wanted copied. I remember Mum often saying how they really believed she could perform miracles, although the extra income made it possible to pay the weekly rent and provide many little extras for us children.

One of my most vivid memories as a child, was laying awake late at night listening to the vibrating sound of the foot operated treadle sewing machine, running seemingly endlessly like a miniature pneumatic drill, throughout the long night. During the day I often watched her hunched over the machine peddling furiously, puffing smoke from a cheap "Woodbine" or "Players Weights" cigarette drooping from the corner of her mouth. The smoke curling up into her eyes caused her to squint, whilst at the same time dexterous fingers guided the material past the rapidly stabbing needle. Finally the long length of ash would drop off and the machine was momentarily silent, as she leaned forward to blow the dust away and then light another almost instantly, before resuming her frantic peddling.

Frequently one of my sisters was sent running to the top of the road, where the local shops were located, with a few coins clutched in a hot little hand to buy a reel of cotton thread from the drapery, or a little flat packet containing five cigarettes from the tobacconists. My sister once described how somewhere between the house and the shops she lost the money, and, after frantically looking for some time, had to return home empty handed. At this time Mum was very poor and often found it hard to make ends meet, as it was I never recalled her getting angry, or physically punishing anyone for such minor accidents. Usually they would be sent straight back to the shop once again, after making sure the money was wrapped in a piece of paper with instructions written down, together with a piece of cloth matching the color of the cotton. The summer and autumn of 1936 following Dad's death, until late November, was a very worrying time for Mum. With six children and no wage earner to provide a steady income and two infants at home every day, something had to be done. Eventually a decision was made, which was obviously very difficult for her and proving disastrous for the four youngest, affecting us for the remainder of our lives.

Eventually it was decided, following a discussion with my Grandfather Herbert Mills, that Yvonne and Joan who were at the time ten and nine years of age and therefore able to help in the house, should stay home. The rest of us, including my brother and two youngest sisters, were to be "Orphaned Out!" How this decision was finally arrived at was not clear at the time and neither did we ever know why the one particular location was chosen. Much later in life we discovered it was again my Grandparents' suggestion, eventually and inevitably causing some dissension among other members of the family that prevailed for many years. My Mother never really discussed it with me or explained the exact reasons, except to say that at the time there really was no other choice.

Vague snatches of the grey, drizzly November day, when we were finally taken away from home still spring to mind. Recollections of the bus ride to the center of London and train journey from Euston Station to the City of Birmingham are hazy, as is the final stretch into the Warwickshire countryside near the town of Sutton Coldfield, where our new home was destined to be for many years to come.

Most of the tiresome journey was spent looking out the misted window of the third class carriage, watching telegraph poles and trees flash by, with occasional glimpses of farmhouses and hayfields through rain spattered windows. On the seat opposite to me my brother lay asleep with his head on Mum's lap, at the time oblivious to the drama unfolding. Eventually the hissing, screeching, monster of a train pulled into the noisy, smoke-blackened City of Birmingham's New Street Station, a scene remembered for the remainder of my life.

A double-decker "Midland Red" Bus with a low, flat platform at the back and an open winding metal staircase leading to the upper deck carried us out of the city and into the suburbs. A short walk along Chester Road from the bus stop led us to the Nursery School, a large imposing Victorian red brick building, with extending, bay wooden framed windows and a high arched front doorway. As we approached the shadowy entrance along the graveled driveway flanked by lawn and bushes, sudden fear overwhelmed me and I clung tightly to Mums' hand.

Upon entering we were asked to wait in a dingy stone-tiled hall-way, sitting on a long wooden seat that stretched the complete width of deep bay windows. After a few moments a short, plump little old lady entered from a side door, her face deeply wrinkled and graying red hair drawn into a tight ball at the back of her head. Her ankle length, dark blue dress was high-buttoned to the neck, with a stiff white collar and broad matching cuffs at the wrists. On top of her head a flat matching blue bonnet was pinned, flopping precariously to one side as she walked. We were informed this person was Sister Fanny, Head Sister of the Nursery, responsible for all infants and younger children residing there.

It is now difficult to remember much of the ensuing conversation, other than being firmly informed that Maurice and I would be staying there temporally, while Pauline and Audrey, apparently, were to reside across the road in one of the girl's houses in the "Main Branch" of the Children's Home.

"We don't want them to live somewhere else!" Pauline complained loudly. "Why can't we stay together?"

Up to that point I had not known exactly what was happening and suddenly became very scared, realizing we were about to lose our loving sisters who had always protected us.

"Why?" I tearfully questioned; "Why can't we be together?"

At that moment my Mother tried to explain it would only be for a "little while" and we would "soon make a lot of new friends," but I didn't see it that way. When my Father had passed away it had not meant very much to me, probably because I was too young to know, but now I was suddenly very aware of what was happening and did not like it at all! Both Maurice and I broke into sobbing cries, when without warning our hands were released and remaining family members hurriedly headed for the door.

Looking pathetically down at us Mum unconvincingly remarked; "Be good boys! We will see you soon!" Two expressions I would remember for a very long time.

In the next moment they were gone and strange firm arms held us back, as the solid front door slammed shut behind them. Sitting alone together on the window seat Maurice and I peered through the drizzling rain running down the glass, as they walked slowly away from the house and disappeared into the late afternoon November mist. Our first night in strange beds and unfamiliar surroundings, we both eventually cried ourselves to a lonely restless sleep.

Many years later Mum recalled how she had looked back to see us tearfully looking out the window. "A scene that became indelible in her memory". At the time we were totally unaware that the next few months at the Nursery would, in fact, turn out to be the happiest and most enjoyable since leaving home. Sister Fanny would eventually prove to be the single most thoughtful and caring person I would come to know for almost the next decade. As Head Sister, with help from a small staff of aides and "apprentice" senior girls from the home, she supervised all daily routines including meals, play and both elementary education and religious indoctrination.

After the initial shock and sorrow at leaving home had worn off, we both gradually settled down and in time eventually became accustomed to our new surroundings and the nursery-home routine. Infants and children between the ages of two and five lived in the converted Victorian Mansion until they were old enough to be transferred to one of the houses in the main Orphanage, a short distance away. Maurice, who was not yet three, had to stay for over two years, whereas I was transferred after only a few months. The exact number of infant children in the home was unclear to me at the time, but every member of the staff was kind and attentive to our every need. All meals were taken at little round tables, where we sat in low straight-backed chairs in the dining room, approached from the wide entrance hall. There were a total of four tables with an equal number of the pastel painted chairs set around each one.

Highly polished dark wooden planks had been laid on the floors in most rooms, although some boasted a gaily-colored, Indian-style carpet in the center. One exception was the playroom, where tall toy lockers covered one wall. Sometime later my brother had a nasty accident while attempting to climb up to the top shelf to reach a toy, when the handle he was standing on broke off exposing a long screw that gashed his thigh as he fell. Unfortunately, in the near future, he would again prove to be a little accident-prone!

A wide, carpeted staircase wound upstairs to brightly wall-papered bedrooms. Each one large enough to accommodate four tiny iron-framed beds arranged side by side, provided for older children who did not require sides. Younger infants were placed in wooden, high-framed cots and slept in a separate, smaller room, further along the broad upper landing.

Most rooms in the house were suitably decorated with a neat child's décor, so it didn't take long before we began to feel "at home", although frequently there were still times we both missed our Mother and sisters. Thankfully we still had each other to turn to for comfort, whenever or wherever pangs of occasional homesickness befell either of us, which for me was frequently at night beneath the bedcovers.

Behind the Nursery a large garden area with shrubs, fruit trees and tennis courts was located, where we often sat on sunny days to watch the adults play. Smaller children, including my brother, were encouraged to take naptime in the afternoon on little canvas cots, placed in rows out on the lawn. Located further back was a long shaded meadow with mature oak trees, where many years later as a Boy Scout I returned to enjoy camping.

At that time I became one of a small troop of uniformed youths pushing a two wheeled, flat- topped cart, loaded with tents and camping equipment, along Chester Road from The Orphanage, returning to the familiar grounds for a weekend camp, where once more we enjoyed the scent of tall grasses and wild flowers, bringing back earlier more pleasant memories. The occasion was one of a very small number of enjoyable interludes experienced during the long monotonous years following my earlier stay at the nursery.

To this day I still remember the Boy Scout song, sung with such gusto on our way to the familiar campgrounds, as follows;

"We are the ninety second. We know our manners.

We spend our tanners (sixpence) we are expected wherever we go.

As we go marching along the road, doors and windows open wide, wide, wide.

Hi-tiddly-hi-ti, eat brown bread. Ever see a sausage fall down dead?

We are the Ninety Second"!

[We were known as the Ninety Second Birmingham Boy Scout Troop.]

Following an-all-to-brief-time spent in the friendly atmosphere of the Nursery School, eventually yet another period of separation was to be endured.

In March of 1937 Neville Chamberlain was Prime Minister and a number of historically significant events took place in England. King Edward the Duke of Windsor abdicated from the throne, following his broadcast from Windsor Castle. His brother the Duke of York was crowned King George the Sixth in a ceremony six months later, and the British Broadcasting Company began the first television broadcasts from Alexander Palace in London. The most memorable event for me that year, however, occurred shortly after my fifth birthday, when eventually the time came for me to leave my brother and the kind Head Sister Fanny, to be taken across and placed in one of the houses for boys in the "Main Branch".

"At least I will be able to see my sisters again" I contemplated, but it did not quite work out the way anticipated!

2

The Home

"Princess Alice Orphanage" the sign read in large gold colored letters, set in a black ornamental wrought iron frame, arching high over a graveled entrance leading to the main administrative offices. The building adjoined an imposing church with a central bell tower, displaying a round white-faced clock with black pointed hands, clearly visible from the ground. On either side set at right angles but attached to the main buildings were two identical houses, which I later discovered were the residences of the Governor, Mr. Jacka, and the Assistant Governor at the time, Mr. Roycroft. Most of the buildings were completed at the turn of the century in a typical Victorian style of red brick, with solid oak supports above the wooden framed doors and windows. Similar to the church, all the roofs were laid with hundreds of grey slates sloping up to tall brick chimney stacks, topped with little round red clay funnels. The whole impressive office block faced the center of an expansive mowed green oval, surrounded on three sides by similarly constructed houses. Each one was approached by a separate, smaller walkway, connected to a wide concrete drive which encircled the entire green.

Across the oval, facing the clock tower stood the hospital, built of lighter colored bricks with rows of wide, light metal framed windows and a railed balcony on a flat roof overlooking a play area with swings and a see-saw. It was altogether a more modern looking building than the stern, forbidding houses that flanked the other two sides. To the right of the hospital, a two storied brick cottage boasted a wood and glass "conservatory type" front entrance, where older girls lived who attended high school. The cottage was named Ajax, although the connection was never discovered.

Completing the circle, were rows of tall houses also characteristically Victorian in design, with wood framed windows and doors painted a dark green. On one side stood four houses for girls named Shaftsbury, Copely, Icknield and Jevons, while opposite, the boy's residences were titled March, Seymour, Meriden, Beatrice and Wand.

Most of them presumably named after predominant personages or wealthy benefactors, none of whom I am certain, were ever aware of the childhood miseries endured by so many within those "blessed" walls.

Situated behind the boy's houses the playing fields were used, depending on the season, for either soccer or cricket. Nearly every Saturday a game took place between different house teams or "Princess Alice and a "Visitors" team. Alongside the fields, separated by a path to the back entrance, stood two wooden storage sheds and a cricket pavilion, used for storing sports equipment and machinery to mark out and maintain the playing areas. These buildings were to prove very useful at a future date as somewhere to hide.

Playing soccer and cricket in those early years, together with running the "Hundred Yard Dash" on "Sports Days," was a memorable time, when the entire area was magically turned overnight into a huge festive fairground, with striped tents and hundreds of fluttering flags. Whenever the "home" was open to the public we enjoyed much greater freedom, and on the few "Sports Days" or the Annual Fete on the front oval, we forgot our somber surroundings and the strict discipline for a while and behaved like normal happy children. It was almost as if the "Sisters" took the opportunity on these occasions, to show off to visitors how kind and considerate they always were to their young charges.

If one were experienced enough to represent the house in a sport, you were considered quite a hero, so my brother and I were therefore often fortunate to be picked regularly for a team, because in spite of our slight stature we both could "run like the devil." In later years personally benefiting greatly from my participation in sports and my close friendship with many of the players, who came to compete against us from outside, although at the time with no inkling of just how much their friendship would mean.

Behind the houses where the girls lived on the opposite side of The Green, were cultivated grounds where vegetables, flowers and different shrubs grew. Known as the "Gardens," they surrounded two long glass covered greenhouses, which later suffered a wartime bombing fate. In the gardens long rows of damson and apple trees grew, where as a junior schoolboy I was caught and severely punished for "Scrumping!" A local vernacular commonly used for stealing apples. Alongside the gardens stood two black wooden, oblong huts, elevated on short brick piers and approached by a narrow gravel path, used by Girl Guides and Boy Scouts on alternative evenings after school and also, at times, for choir practices.

Years later I was to meet kind Sister Fanny from the Nursery School once again in her other position as the church organist, loudly thumping out music being rehearsed by choir members for the annual Christmas Concert. At one of these rehearsals discovering she wore a ginger wig, when the hair-piece suddenly slipped back over her head to reveal wispy grey hair, as she flung up her arms to emphasize a high note I was straining to reach. Even though only nine at the time I remember the song very well, because it reflected my own feelings exactly at that moment and for long afterwards.

The lyrics expressed! "O for the wings, for the wings of a dove. Far away, Far away would I fly"!

I often wished many times to have just been able to fly away!

Close to the Governors House and Church stood the brick Bakery, containing huge cast iron gas fired ovens and broad wooden tables where the dough was pounded. The hand-rolled sausage-like white dough was placed on flat trays and pushed onto the heated metal plates with long wooden handled spatulas. The loaves were later removed, crusty brown and steaming hot, emitting a wonderful sweet aroma to be arranged on the flat, white scrubbed tables to cool. Both Maurice and I worked in the Bakery at different times as unpaid apprentices, forming part of a regular schedule with boys from different houses

Next to the Bakery, the Laundry Room housed giant silver metal steam boilers and vast open washtubs, positioned next to jaw-like presses. Rows of heavy, hand held flat irons, heated on cast iron wood burning stoves were used to press linens and garments for the houses and hospital. The Bakery and Laundry also "employed" older girls and boys as apprentice trainees, working shifts with paid staff recruited from outside. Both my sisters as pre-teenagers, spent many hours working in the laundry as pressers and sorters. Pauline labored endlessly on the giant cloth-covered roller presses, operated by steam and used for ironing bed sheets. At one time her hands almost became trapped as she smoothed the sheet, nearly dragging her into the scolding hot, unrelenting rollers.

A little way from the laundry yet another tall brick building covered the swimming pool, open only in the summertime. Normally there was strict segregation of boys and girls, except when there was a competition with teams coming in from outside.

When learning to swim boys were pulled along the edge of the pool by a rope looped under their armpits, with the trainer at the other end running and yelling instructions.

Frequently gulping and spluttering out the horrible chlorinated water, I eventually learned to swim quite well, even jumping off the springboard to "bomb" others in the water.

In the winter the pool was covered with a wooden floor where girls played netball, (similar to basketball). Whereas boys were separately coached in gymnastics on wall bars, beams and a leather-covered vaulting horse. The Coach frequently praised me for my athletic ability and suggested I should pursue the sport later in life, although the opportunity never came until many years later as a boy soldier.

Two detached brick cottages were located close to a separate farm entrance, where the baker, Mister Salt and the head gardener lived.

The path led past the cottages down a long gravel road extending to the furthest perimeter of the grounds, winding through meadows and cropland before entering the farmyard, where the solid gray stone farmhouse and corrugated iron roofed outbuildings were flanked by squat, oval topped haystacks.

The farm supplied almost all the needs of each household on a daily basis, including milk, vegetables and potatoes. During the war that followed this was obviously a blessing, particularly with the introduction of rationing, when most citizens were encouraged to "grow their own" in allotments. Numerous fruit trees grew on the farm, including pears and plums, which again I was tempted to steal in the future. Some of the Sisters in charge of the houses bottled and preserved these fruits, storing them on marble shelves in the cool pantries. However, it was seldom any of the boys sampled them, although once I managed to steal a jar of plums, only to suffer a violent tummy-ache from the unaccustomed sour fruit.

Animals kept on the farm, included cows for milking, chickens, pigs, and two heavy "work horses" used for pulling the great wood-framed, steel bladed plough and hay wagons. Endless hours were spent watching those great magnificent beasts blowing hot air from their nostrils, straining to turn the deep furrows of soil, while overhead blackbirds circled and cawed on late autumn days. A smaller breed of horse was also regularly harnessed to a lighter cart or "milk float," used to deliver fresh milk contained in tall stainless steel churns, carefully stacked in the back.

Outside each house a white enamel pail with a flat lid was placed by the front door and at each stop the farmer dipped a thin handled ladle into the churn, doling out a required number, depending on the total occupants. Similarly the baker placed bread and pastry goods on the step, delivered from a hand-propelled three-wheeled box cart.

Both the farmer and baker used boys appointed to help them deliver on their early morning rounds. These were much sought after chores, as one was often rewarded with a drink of cool fresh milk or allowed to chomp on a currant bun, usually only intended for the sisters' table. Later, during his confinement in Seymour House, my brother was one of those fortunate enough to be so employed.

After the "milk round" was completed, the farmer turned the horse out to pasture in the meadow behind the hospital. Frequently after school, as I made my way down to the field, I enjoyed climbing on the patient equine "bareback," clinging to the mane while he meandered and grazed. Seldom did he object, except occasionally breaking into a trot before suddenly lowering his head to tumble me laughing into the long grass.

Unknowingly this was probably my first introduction to the hazards of horseback riding that eventually led me onto much greater equestrian pursuits in the future.

A narrow alley behind the assistant governor's house separated the first boys' house March from the Primary School, where my youngest sister Pauline once had another unfortunate accident, when a heavy slate blackboard fell on her head one day knocking her unconscious and leaving a permanent scar. Children from the age of five attended the infant school until they were old enough to be sent to the Boldmere Secondary Modern School, located a couple of miles outside The Orphanage grounds, a distance all students walked in pairs every day.

Surrounding the children's Primary School, a solid red stonewall and high metal railings separated two black tarmac playgrounds. Outside the schoolyard was an area known as the "top playground," used by older boys for various games such as yard football or wall cricket when stumps were drawn on the wall with chalk. At the far end of the yard stood a low brick, red tiled building containing rows of squat toilet cubicles, facing a line of metal troughed urinals. An open doorway at each end proved useful in later years as an escape route from the keen-scented omnipresent Mr Brassington, when some of the more adventurous teens indulged in the evils of tobacco. One was not considered a man until having taken the first spluttering puff from a filthy little "dog end" one of the older boys had retrieved somewhere, an evil practice that became almost a form of initiation into the "Big Boys Club" and, unfortunately, a habit lasting well into the future. In the center of the playground stood a massive "Horse Chestnut Tree," encircled by high black wrought iron railings curving outward to a point at the top, intending to deter boys from climbing.

At least that was the intention but it almost caused my brother's death in later years, when he attempted to climb up to collect some of the prickly coated "conkers," (another local vernacular) and fell missing the sharp railings by inches, only to shatter his leg on the hard tarmac below. Around the huge thick trunk and protruding tentacles of roots, a low- built grey stone wall, anchoring the railings, was frequently used as a shady seat for swapping cigarette cards or other collectibles. It was also useful as an easy step up for the more adventurous, who were daring enough to attempt the treacherous ascent.

Brampton Hall, a high roofed brick building adjoining the Primary School hosted a variety of gatherings during each year but was mainly used for school assembly or sometimes doubled as another gymnasium, or even on special occasions for concerts, especially the annual Christmas Party. The hall was entered either through an adjoining passageway from the school or by an outside double door from the playground. Inside, set off to one side of the stage, was a room where Mister Brassington occupied an office. We were never quite certain of his exact staff position but very soon he became known as "The Discipline Master," invariably doling out prescribed punishment. Unfortunately it was my destiny to have a number of desperate encounters with him, at a future date.

Meriden House, the first I was sent to and remained for the duration, was named after a town located in almost the exact center of England. It stood in the middle of a row of five boys' houses facing the large green oval. At the rear a narrow path separated each house from the playing fields, blocked by a row of bunkers, where each individual house stored coke or fuel required for heating the boilers, burning in open fireplaces or black, wrought-iron cooking stoves. Both front and back doors of Meriden House opened into a long connecting hallway dividing the house and extending the full length. On one side were bathrooms, cloakroom and pantry, with the sisters' sitting room situated forward by the front door. On the opposite side of the corridor, starting at the rear, were the "boot room", dining hall and a spacious "Playroom," boasting a wood block floor and rows of small cubbyholes for keeping toys, each individual space visibly numbered at the top. Ascending from the hallway a wide stepped staircase, with a solid wooden banister led up to the first floor landing. At the top of the stairs was the first bedroom where I slept practically every night for the next decade. The room contained ten little iron framed beds, five either side, spaced a few feet apart with a round, white glazed chamber pot peeking from under the bed nearest the door.

Every bed was covered similarly with a patterned, thin cotton "counterpane" spread, laid over two bright red blankets and starched white sheets which always felt damp and cold. Two solid cast-iron radiators set against the wall were invariably cold, or at best lukewarm, providing the only heat in the room.

Unlike the nursery, recently moved from, most of the rooms used by boys were very sparsely furnished, appearing vast and uninviting, conveying an instant feeling of apprehension and despair. These concerns were never shed until well into the future and certain rooms I dreaded entering even up until the final day of leaving. Not only because of the emptiness or the somber, drab colors of the walls, but a pervading feeling of extreme loneliness and fear of an unknown fate. It became obvious shortly after my arrival, never to expect sympathy or comfort from certain individual staff members. Tears were ignored and one soon learnt to suppress emotions until the shelter of a dark and lonely bed permitted a private, night-time silent sob.

Every morning at six we rose and immediately remade beds, neatly folding the top sheet over the blanket, pulling the bedspread over the pillow and folding neat "hospital corners" at the bottom, a practice that stood me in good stead later in life after joining the Army. Nightshirts were also neatly folded and placed under the pillow, unless of course, they were urine soiled, unfortunately a frequent occurrence by younger inmates, instantly reportable to the sister on duty and incurring stern and embarrassing consequences.

All bedrooms and landing floors, except for the Sisters, were covered in light brown shiny linoleum, which owing to years of wear and constant polishing by generations of young boys had become extremely slippery, particularly when wearing thick woolen socks. In some places the shiny covering was worn out, exposing bare wooden floorboards with sharp protruding splinters, frequently causing minor but painful injury.

Across the landing a few feet away was the Head Sister's bedroom, which during all the years spent living in Meriden I was never privileged to have more than a brief glimpse into. On one rare occasion when the door was open in my presence, I only saw part of a multi-patterned carpet with solid, dark wooden furniture placed in front of heavily draped windows.

Further down the landing toward the back of the house the linen and clothes closets were installed, positioned alongside the staff bathroom and the assistant Sisters bedroom.

On the opposite side was a bedroom smaller than the one at the front with fewer beds, where older boys usually slept. Unfortunately that particular privilege was never to be enjoyed by me.

Yet another narrower staircase ascended to the third floor attic, used mainly for storage of mysterious boxes and suitcases in a dark cobwebbed cupboard at the far end. This part of the house was declared "out of bounds" normally and was thought to be a very scary place, particularly by new boys, as it was nearly always the place where one was dared to go at night, whenever a game of "Truth or Dare" was played. This game was often enjoyed after being sent to bed and invariably involved someone getting into trouble if caught, obviously heightening the excitement and tension.

The only other room on this floor was the "Pressing" or "Drying Room," so named because clothes and linens were taken there for airing after washing and ironing. At times however it was known as the "Isolation Room," where anyone sick with an infectious childhood illness was isolated until they recovered. For this purpose mainly, there was a high double bunk-bed with an iron frame in the center of the room, facing a small barred window set in a gable, close to the apex of the roof. Nearly every room in the house eventually provided a particular memory, some good, others bad but the Isolation Room was hated very early on and despised until the day of my eventual hasty departure.

Beyond the last boys' house, "Wand," was a long sloping grass bank leading down to yet another tarmac-covered "Bottom Playground," where a spacious, high roofed shelter stood with an open front. Inside a few feet above the ground, running the whole length of the building was a thick wooden bench, engraved with hundreds of carved initials and figures dating back almost to the start of the century. A common practice over the years to while away the time was to gouge them into the wood, with whatever sharp implement one could find, and eventually my own and my brother's initials were added to those already imbedded.

At the bottom of the grassy slope, facing the shelter, an abandoned shell of an old rusty motorcar sat, with the engine and seat upholstery long since removed. Forlorn on its wheel-less hubs it still retained a steering wheel, gear and brake levers. Many fun-filled hours were spent playing in the wreck, with imaginations carrying us to far away places or racing at the famous Silverstone Speedway with famous English race car drivers like John Cobb or Sir Donald Campbell.

Next to the lower playground behind the hospital and senior girls' cottage, a large expanse of meadowland was fenced by low iron railings, where farm horses and cows were frequently turned out to graze. As a young teen many happy hours were spent in this pasture, carefully avoiding the "cow packs," lying in the long grass chewing on sweet-and-sour tasting "vinegar leaves" growing in abundance. They were seldom found anywhere else and the actual name of the weed was never personally diagnosed, but the bittersweet taste was almost addictive and eagerly searched for as a form of confection.

The exact acreage of The Orphanage was always a mystery to me but at a young impressionable age it appeared as a vast colorful world of meadows, farmland and gardens, crisscrossed with endless tracks and pathways that often mentally carried me far away from the grey, uninviting buildings. The houses by comparison appeared stark and imposing, very seldom during my stay was there ever a sense of comfort or warmth within their solid walls.

All the boys feared Sister Eileen Holloway, the Head Sister in charge of Meriden House, and under her care it was not long before I also began to fear her. Upon arrival at the age of five there was not very much to worry about, at first my treatment was rather special like all new arrivals, but the privilege soon ended as I grew up and new younger boys arrived.

Before very long I ceased calling her "Sister", except to her face, and began to use the title all the other boys used. Soon discovering "The Rat," was a very suitable nick name for this sister for various reasons. Standing very tall and skinny with sharp facial features exaggerated by a long pointed nose and thin mean lips, deep sunken dark eyes peered out from below a short black fringe covering most of her forehead. At the back of her head hair was cut short, exposing a shaved white neck protruding above the stiff white collar of a starched navy-blue uniform. Not only her appearance, however, earned the nickname but also the apparent ability to hear so acutely every sound, particularly at night. Her sharp vision seldom missed anything she was not supposed to see. In fact nothing, at any time ever escaped "The Rat's" notice.

Sister Eva her assistant, on the other hand, was compassionate and at times friendly and quite understanding, which may have had something to do with her not having been at the home for very long? Born in Wales her voice reflected the musical accent, so much softer and more pleasing to the ear, unlike the harsh, bitter tone we had grown accustomed to.

Although none of us ever knew either of their ages, it was obvious that Sister Eva was much younger so most of the boys felt comfortable in confiding in her, feeling able to communicate and seldom getting into trouble when she was on duty. If anyone in the home ever became a "Mother Figure" it was her and I always regretted not having the opportunity to meet again and thank her for so many comforting times. To this day recalling her shoulder length, light colored hair, pulled back from a kindly face, with bright blue eyes that softened as she spoke, reminding me very much at the time of my eldest sister Yvonne. Shorter in stature than "The Rat," Sister Eva obviously possessed a much larger heart and often tried to reach out to us, but was all-too-often prevented from doing so. Life at "The Home" was on numerous occasions made so much more bearable by her presence and rare sympathetic understanding of the needs of all the youngsters in her care.

Seldom did we leave the home grounds alone, usually only to walk the few miles to school in pairs or be taken for a group walk by one of the sisters in the park on Sundays. Although occasionally, growing up, I became bolder and often sneaked out with a friend across the Chester Road to the "Tuck Shop," to scrounge for broken biscuits or over-ripe fruit from The Greengrocer. Frequently we had to hastily return through the back playing field entrance, or a hole in the fence, to avoid being nabbed with our bounty by a member of staff.

Outside close to the massive round-a-bout at the junction of Chester and Jockey roads was the "Beggars Bush" Public House, a prominent imposing building with lofty bay curtained windows and a sloping green copper roof. In front of the public bar entrance, a tall colorful sign bearing a picture of a bedraggled, bearded beggar and the name, swung on a high wooden frame. Later, during the war because of rationing, the number of residents and uniformed visitors who frequented the establishment often surprised me. Obviously the ingredients used in brewing the local ale were still readily available, providing ample calorific sustenance to regulars as well as the large number of American servicemen who frequented the pub during opening hours.

Adjoining the pub a high stone wall half hid an overgrown garden and gray brick building, known by the boys as the "Hermit's House." Close to the wall, visible through a wrought-iron gate, stood a rustic, log-planked shed with a corrugated iron roof. At one end a thick wooden door was centered between two small framed windows set on either side.

It was impossible to see through owing to years of caked-on dust and grime, but it created great speculation as to what went on inside.

Older boys flouted numerous rumors describing a mysterious, bearded tramp-like figure, supposedly seen entering and leaving at dawn and dusk. Nobody really knew and frequent discussions only fueled boyhood imaginations and an innate desire to explore. Naturally there was some hesitation to be the first individual to risk trespassing and discover what really went on inside but finally, after passing the location frequently and suffering constant prodding by others, curiosity prevailed and together with a friend a dare was eventually accepted to investigate.

With difficulty the pair of us managed to scale the wall by digging the toes of our boots into the crumbling crevices between the stones. Then landing on the far side amidst the overgrown brush and weeds, we furtively approached the half-hidden shack and hesitantly pulled at the latch to open the rustic, dilapidated door.

As it creaked slowly ajar we peered around the post into a cobweb-strewn interior, where long rows of wooden shelves ran lengthwise laden with a variety of multicolored clay pots. In the center of the room stood a square marble-topped table, bearing a flat circular shelf revolving on a round iron axle. A wide leather belt extended to a foot treadle through a series of gears, reminding me of the treadle on my mother's sewing machine. Pushing down firmly with my foot the huge wheel slowly began to rotate, gradually accelerating as more pressure was exerted forward and back. Next to the turntable on metal legs, stood a white enameled sink with dull brass colored taps that constantly dripped water onto the rust stained base. On the bottom and sides, dollops of wet red clay, soft and cold to the touch were deposited, making it increasingly obvious what really took place in the shed.

Curiosity satisfied we turned to exit the door, stepping into the bright sunlight as a tall figure suddenly appeared, blocking our path to the gate. It was as if the faded figure from the pub sign had suddenly come to life. Standing petrified not daring to move all manner of thoughts were conjured up, staring at his bearded face framed in long matted grey hair. Escape was impossible, there was no way past him through the thick waist-high weeds, as we stood for what seemed an endless moment motionless, scared he was about to attack and feeling certain he was going to. Then from beneath bushy eyebrows, piercing blue eyes gradually softened and a broad smile changed his whole appearance instantly.

Breathing became easy again as fingernails slowly unclenched from the depths of palms, he didn't look so fierce anymore, just a slightly disheveled old man.

"Well young fellows where did you come from?" His voice soft and kindly, with an accent different to the local dialect I had already begun to adopt.

"We came from outside," I ventured.

"We were lost!" Hoping my answer would suffice.

Soon we blurted out where we actually came from and that we were "exploring" but "how interesting his shed was." Surprisingly we were invited back inside and discovered how all kinds of clay pots for horticultural gardens were made, as he demonstrated how the wet clay was molded on the wheel. Large, sinewy hands delicately shaped the mass of earthen clay into a beautiful design, featuring a slim neck tapering up from a bulbous bottom to a high curved collar. Fascinating to watch we became totally enthralled until finally leaving, as the kindly old man let us out through a black, wrought iron gate, inviting us to "Return anytime we wanted!"

Later back at the home we were able to discount the tales of a "crazy hermit" but unfortunately were never able to make a return visit. During one of the wartime nightly blitzes that followed a stray bomb landed, narrowly missing the pub but completely destroying the old house and severely damaging the pottery shed. It stood derelict for the remainder of the war when eventually the area was cleared for more modern buildings. Sadly the opportunity never came enabling me to see the friendly old artisan again

3

The Cloakroom

"Boys will be Boys!" someone once said and although I was never quite sure what was meant by that, maybe at the time I was one they had in mind. Admittedly perhaps mischievous often but I didn't consider myself naughty, although I was frequently accused of being a "naughty boy!" Most certainly I was not a sissy and never avoided a confrontation when it involved something considered wrong, regardless of whether it was from another boy or a staff member.

However, there was no doubt I resented being in The Orphanage, resented being left by my mother and resented being separated from my brother and sisters. In fact always feeling bitter and hating nearly everyone intent on keeping me there, with only one exception, described later. Feelings never changed from the time of my arrival in 1936, until the day eventually running away over nine years later in 1945.

The most repetitive and fervent thought from earliest memories was how to escape and find my way back home. But how, when and where home even was, worried me for almost a decade of despair. In all likelihood becoming a "naughty boy" because loneliness, resentment and desperation caused me to be naughty!

My brother Maurice, younger by twenty months, finally joined me in Meriden House in 1938, apparently at Mums request. He had continued to stay at the Nursery School across the road from The Orphanage, in the care of Sister Fanny until he was five.

Together once more it became my duty, or perhaps instinct, to protect him from anything or anybody who threatened him. This, of course, frequently meant getting into trouble following arguments or fights with older boys and even with the sisters in charge. Sometimes my "protection" may have been confused with being the "Big Brother," or perhaps just showing off or even responding to a "Dare!" It was common practice for one boy, usually older, to dare a new boy to try something considered naughty or even dangerous, particularly at night when we were supposed to be safely in bed.

On one memorable night shortly before the war, I was punished for creating a disturbance after bedtime. It was considered a cardinal sin to talk or be caught out of bed except for the essentials and if discovered one suffered dire consequences.

None-the-less, boys being boys we often took it in turns to relate in a whisper, ghostly stories to any others still awake. Unfortunately, whispers gradually became louder as the excitement and questions increased. It was obviously too much to ask ten young virile boys to remain silent and not move when sent to bed so early. The moment it was established by a nominated watcher the sisters had retired to their sitting room, the fun began.

One boy named Derek Burt was an expert at telling made up stories, often recounting the most imaginative tales, literally scaring his listeners huddled in the dark, to the point where they crouched in fear or giggled uncontrollably under the bedclothes. The incredible fact was that normally, especially in front of staff, he stuttered uncontrollably, hardly able to put two words together without relapsing into the embarrassing affliction. At night, however, whilst relating hair-raising stories to his young friends, he always spoke slowly and distinctly.

One other boy somehow acquired a "Cats Whisker" crystal boxed radio set, the forerunner of the modern wireless, an early device consisting of wire metal electrodes, which when connected picked up incoming radio signals. A group of us were often invited to join him beneath his tented top sheet, propped up by our heads, to listen with earphones to the hesitant, crackly music and stunted commentaries relayed. For a short while we enjoyed a series of these exciting sessions, until eventually the escapade was discovered by "The Rat", who confiscated the box set and metered out the inevitable punishment, wielding a rubber soled slipper with her usual gusto.

In each room beneath the first bed by the door a chamber pot was positioned and it became a sort of tradition that every new boy should sleep there, until another new arrival guaranteed a move further away. It was never considered a good place to sleep, not only because of the frequent interruptions during the night but also the close proximity of the pervasive odor of urine. The unfortunate individual in this bed also had the unenviable task of listening and keeping watch by the door for the sister's creaky approach up the stairs.

The large porcelain pot became known as the "Gusunder" (goes under) with handles on the side, making it easier to carry downstairs to empty into the toilet at the end of the cloakroom every morning before breakfast. If full, which it invariable was, it required two boys to carry it slowly down the long wooden staircase. On the way it was frequently spilled, most often at the moment of emptying into the toilet bowl, hence the ever-present stench in the cloakroom.

My own "crime," at one particular time, resulted from a late "call to nature". Crawling out of bed to kneel and pulling the pot out from under the first bed, carefully raising my nightshirt to the necessary height, I proceeded to relieve myself, directing the jet carefully towards the center. At first this task had taken some considerable practice before becoming proficient and new boys in particular frequently missed the spot, or pot, especially in the dark. This night was no exception, someone had missed earlier and the surrounding floor area was totally saturated.

Rising to my feet I slipped, kicking the pot, sending the shiny bowl and the entire contents swooshing across the wooden boards. Hearing the commotion, sharp-eared Sister Eileen rushed up the stairs, from whence she probably had been secretly lurking, to find me floundering on the sodden boards in a wringing wet, pee-soaked nightshirt.

"You again boy" She shrieked through clenched teeth, grabbing my ear in her long bony fingers and twisting it viciously.

"Clean this mess up then get down on the stool!"

After mopping it up with the long-handled cloth mop from the bathroom, I retreated to the adjoining cloakroom, where offenders were generally left sitting in the cold and dark for hours until the sisters finally retired, usually following the late night news from the BBC. It wasn't my first instance of being relegated to sitting alone downstairs, since the age of five having frequently suffered the same isolation, shivering and cowering fearful in the dark. By now the experience had become a lot less frightening, being older and more aware over time of insects and creatures that lurked in the night, plus the location of certain prominent fixtures.

As usual it was dark and smelly in the long narrow cloakroom on this particular winter night and perching precariously on top of the high three-legged wooden stool, inside the open doorway, was cold and uncomfortable. Wearing only a thin gray, much washed linen nightshirt, trying to pull my knees up and draw the bottom of the flimsy garment over my legs, only made my backside ache, causing the neck hole to gape sending a nasty cold draught down my front.

The walls were dark brown, wood paneled, without a door to the hallway and small, square, red-stone tiles covered the floor, icy cold under my bare feet. Behind and above my head a single row of large brass, double-ended coat hooks stretched the length of the wall, holding a variety of out-door coats. Above each one a different number signified the owner. In total twenty-four hooks, one for each boy in the house.

Upon arrival at Meriden House my allocated number was seventeen and this number was marked on everything owned, from a toothbrush to the pair of tight, black lace-up boots that always cramped my feet. The system made it clear whether items were replaced correctly after use and woe-betide the offender if they were not!

During the lengthy time at Princess Alice Orphanage it was seldom I wore a pair of boots that actually fitted, except in the summertime, when all boys wore leather open toed sandals without socks.

Feet were often forced into ill-fitting "hand-me-downs," which pain-fully crunched big toes and caused blisters. On the way to school some boys removed them and went barefoot, slinging the boots around their necks by the laces. Our appearances definitely gave additional cause for the nickname, "urchins," bestowed on us by local, better dressed, inhabitants.

Opposite my huddled position rows of wide, deep wooden shelves, starting about chest high, stretched up to the cob-webbed ceiling. Below the shelves were similarly spacious, dark stained drawers with solid black metal handles. At the far end of the cloakroom a flimsy, latched half door opened into a cubicle containing the low squat por-celain toilet with an overhead, chain flushed, cast iron water tank. Whenever anyone sat on the flat wooden lavatory seat both feet were clearly visible, proving useful when one was desperate to go!

The smell from the toilet always permeated the narrow room, in spite of being cleaned daily by one of the boys as a before-school chore! This particular night was no exception, even in the damp, cold night air the strong smell of stale urine was overpowering.

Sitting listening to the howling wind and the mice squeaking in the wainscoting, it wasn't long before completely losing track of the hour and after finger counting the hooks and handles for the umpteenth time, violent shivering overcame me. The shuddering caused me to fall off the three-legged stool as it tipped backwards, sliding on the shiny red tiles and banging my head on the solid wall behind.

My own "outdoor" coat on number seventeen was a short, knee length woolen girl's garment that buttoned on the "wrong" side, with a dark brown velvet collar, much hated. It had once obviously be-longed to a slight, young girl from across The Green who obviously had outgrown it. According to confirmed practice it was handed down to whomever it fitted, regardless of the sex of the new owner. Pulling the coat off the peg and wrapping it around my shoulders I drew up my knees, hooking my bare toes over the foot rail. The physical effort briefly warming me but soon the chilled feeling returned along with sudden violent muscle cramps.

Standing up and moving around cautiously, as it was forbidden to leave the cloakroom once you had been sent down, I very carefully peered around the doorway into the dim hallway leading toward the front of the house. A venturesome mouse scurried across the tiles from the dining hall opposite, disappearing under the door of the pantry, causing me to vaguely wonder if he would find anything to eat. Lights showed under the sisters' sitting room door and the sound of classical music was occasionally interrupted by their voices. One could visualize them both sitting in armchairs darning socks or sewing whilst listening to the radio, which was their normal routine most evenings, once they thought all boys were safely in bed. Periodically they would take turns to creep to the bottom of the stairs to listen and hopefully catch anyone talking, or worse, out of bed. Usually this practice was counteracted by the boy, previously nominated, who knelt close to the bedroom door to listen and warn of any stealthy approach by a whispered "Cave!" Where-upon everyone dove hurriedly back to bed. However, this pre-caution did not always work, particularly with the deft creeping ability of "The artful Rat!"

Invariably one of us was caught, usually the slowest to get back, who usually suffered either six, sharp stinging whacks on a bare bottom with the black, rubber gym shoe or alternatively sent downstairs to sit in freezing isolation.

Becoming more accustomed to the dark, noticeable, stacked on high deep shelves, piles of what appeared to be curtains or dustsheets were neatly folded in rows above wide wooden drawers. Inquisitively I managed to slide one open, tugging at the black iron handles until finally able to look inside. There was an overpowering smell of mothballs but the space was empty.

At this particular time, just before the outbreak of war, my stature was still quite slight, weighing very little, so removing one of the thick cloth bundles from the shelf above I managed to lay it flat, folding one end into a tight, pillow-like roll. After removing my coat and hanging it back on the peg, very gingerly I attempted to climb up over the edge into the bottom of the deep drawer. By bending both knees slightly and rolling on one side it enabled me to wrap myself in the folds of cloth, resting my head on a large rolled bundle. Inch by inch I managed to pull the drawer closed by wriggling my body inwards, tugging at the edge with the tips of my fingers, until only a very small gap remained. Warm once again snuggling down to doze off, while the hours unknowingly flashed by. Suddenly loud shouts awoke me.

"Boy! Boy! Where are you? Are you hiding? "You had better come out!"

Forgetting my confined location for a moment and attempting to sit up I struck my head sharply on the shelf above, spluttering "Ouch!" The drawer was slowly pulled open revealing my prone figure, looking up blinking sleepily into a bright light. Angrily a voice hissed, "How did you get in there you horrible little boy, we have been looking for you for hours. Get down!"

Climbing awkwardly out of my refuge, standing half asleep on the cold stone floor, I confronted the flashlight-wielding sister.

Grabbing one ear in her usual way with long bony fingers, she exclaimed:

"Do you realize what time it is?" Of course, the exact time was of no concern to me.

"Get up to your room and don't let me hear another sound. We will discuss this affair in the morning!"

Gratefully stumbling up the stairs, assisted by sharp prods from the flashlight I climbed into my little iron bed, ignoring the muffled, boyish giggles from around the room, thinking to myself. "Maybe she will forget by morning!" knowing unfortunately that Head Sister never forgot anything.

Next morning after the usual breakfast of lukewarm cocoa, grey porridge and chunk of plain bread, while getting ready for school I was summoned to the boot room and commanded to "Fetch the slipper!" Once again I was destined to experience the long, thin rubber soled, black gym shoe, kept on a high shelf and used exclusively as a form of punishment for minor offences.

"Bend over!" she directed, proceeding to weigh in with six sharp vicious whacks on my backside, painfully stinging the flesh, even through my thin threadbare short trousers.

"Next time stay on the stool!" she admonished.

After the "hidden" incident I was never sent down to the cloakroom again, however, Sister Eileen was never short of fiendish ideas and before long I was once more the object of her individual attention.

The playroom at the front of the house was situated across the hall from the sisters' sitting room, closer than the cloakroom and more spacious. Most days after returning from school or at weekends, particularly if it was raining, boys played games together or individually with their own toys kept in little numbered lockers. Playtime was a privilege to be taken away at any time and frequently was, for any infringement of the rules. At night the room was very dark, cold and eerie, even the toys which gave so much pleasure to their owners during the day, seemed to change into creepy monsters in the half-light. After my disappearing episode in the cloakroom it was decided that in future, any night-time offenders would be isolated in the playroom until the sisters retired. However, this type of punishment was considered so much better than sitting on the stool in the draughty cloakroom, because at least one was able to lie down.

A thin Hessian mattress was kept rolled beneath the low wooden wall bench, just behind the door and if caught misbehaving in any way the offender was sent down to lie on it. Without a pillow or blanket it was necessary to crook an arm under your head and lay either sideways or flat on your stomach with your arms bent up. Neither of these positions remained very comfortable for long in the confined space under the seat and once again, because of frequent users over a period of time, the mattress was thoroughly permeated with a considerable variety of stale odors and infested with unwelcome "foreign bodies," making the long nights particularly uncomfortable. There was a frequent in-house ritual, however, involving dusting with flea powder and shaving heads for lice. Another common ailment affecting boys was tapeworms, diagnosed and treated in the cottage hospital along with many other recurring childhood afflictions.

Alone in the dark in such an airy room at night often conjured up all kinds of imaginary images, causing repeated attempts to crawl even further under the bench, hugging the wall as close as possible for added security. In this position, through the narrow gap left by the door hinges, one could listen for hours to the radio the sisters invariably had turned on in their sitting room. Before and during the war the BBC broadcast music, plays and commentaries of major sporting events, particularly soccer, cricket and boxing. One particular match recalled was between the famous world heavyweight American champion Joe Louis and the Welshman Tommy Farr. At certain regular hours, an announcer read the news and their names became familiar to me throughout the war. "This is the BBC Home Service. Here is the news, read by Alvar Liddell." Frank Philips, John Snagg or Stuart Hibbard," just some of the names recalled. There were also certain memorable news items such as the Prime Minister Neville Chamberlain's well-known "Peace in our Time" speech and the subsequent declaration of war against Germany in 1939. Radio Shows like "In town tonight," "Music Hall," or dance orchestras such as Geraldo, Ambrose or Billy Cotton. Artists like Gracie Fields or Vera Lynn, whose song "The White Cliffs of Dover" always reminded me of my mother who was born in that town, or "We'll meet again," which meant so much to the thousands of British servicemen sent abroad and also had a similar meaning for me. One particular well known vocalist, remembered for his wonderful deep bass voice, was the African American performer Paul Robeson, who sang "Going Home." Yet another phrase that influenced me.

There were two wooden box type radios in the house, one in the sisters' sitting room and the other placed on the long dresser shelf next to the cocoa urn, in the dining room. This radio was only turned on at special times, such as for "The King's Christmas Day Broadcast" or during the war when we all gathered to listen enthralled to many of Winston Churchill's now famous speeches, which nearly always followed the hourly news.

Whenever relegated to the confines of the playroom, most of the time was spent lying half awake in the cramped space, enjoying an endless variety of classical and patriotic music by Elgar, Coates and even Beethoven or Wagner. Why so much German music was broadcast on the home service during the war made me wonder. Realizing now however, that the long, lonely periods listening in the dark probably helped me develop a deeper appreciation for the classics, although at the time I had absolutely no idea how the music would affect me in later years. Lying alone behind the door, virtually in touch with the whole world through the wonderful new media of "wireless," certainly helped to make the punishment bearable and often almost enjoyable. The music carried me mentally to imaginary places, far, far away from the austere and depressing surroundings relegated to. If the Sisters had only known just how much pleasure was derived from those sessions, most certainly they would have remanded me to a more confined, austere location even earlier. But much worse was destined to follow.

News from other houses spread quickly by word of mouth, particularly when it involved a relative or friend other boys knew. On the way to school, or playing outside, boys and girls swapped information about certain incidents happening in their individual houses. It was not surprising therefore, about this time news was received informing me that my younger sister, Pauline, had suffered an extremely frightening experience at the hands of Sister Flora Ruck, who was in charge of the girl's house, Shaftsbury.

It had not taken long to discover that an acceptable form of punishment in most houses, even those for girls, was that if you were caught talking or misbehaving in any way after "lights out," you were sent down to stay on your own in some cold, dark corner similar to those just described.

At the time of this particular incident Pauline was nearly ten, but even as a younger girl she had always been extremely fearful of the dark. Being banished into an empty unlit room and having the door locked was, to her, a most terrifying experience indeed, eventually diagnosed as "Acute Nyctophobia."

Left alone in this particular circumstance for a considerable length of time, fear finally gave way to loud hysterical, high-pitched screams, which, of course, brought the Sister running to open the door. Then, instead of trying to calm and perhaps quell her hysteria by comfort or a modicum of concern, further punishment was resorted to, reminiscent of the treatment reserved for patients at some mental institutions existing at the time. Forcibly dragging her screaming down the hallway to the bathroom, Pauline was dumped unceremoniously into a tub full of freezing water! Needless to say this archaic ritual did little to quell her panic or overcome an innate fear of the dark, lasting well into the future.

Fortunately that particular form of barbaric treatment was never inflicted on me, learning very early to stifle my emotions and fears. However, some of the other disciplinary methods frequently used against boy offenders were, without doubt, just as cruel and abusive. Certainly the severity of the punishment invariably did not fit the childish nature of the crime. Realization came very early on that female staff in other houses resorted to their own individual methods of instilling discipline and religious beliefs, with little or no regard for age, sex, family or ethnic background.

Other more brutal or exacting forms of punishment were also doled out by senior male administrators, including the "Discipline Master" and Governor, for deliberate infringement of rules or 'ungodly acts' against staff, described in later chapters.

4

Porridge

Entering from the back entrance of the house the dining hall was on the right, thick double doors opened into a long rectangular room with the usual red tiled floor and dark wooden wall panels. On one side, looking out to the playing fields high bay windows extended almost to the ceiling, rising from a low wooden ledge frequently used as a viewing seat.

Inside, to the right of the doors set against the back wall, a solid oak dresser was built in with deep shelves and drawers containing cutlery and crockery. On the bottom wider shelf a tall metal urn, filled with cocoa, was carefully placed every morning just before seven o'clock ready for breakfast. When full it needed two boys to carry it from the kitchen and lift up onto the sideboard, but even then the contents frequently spilled, bringing swift, back-handed retribution from the head sister. Alongside the cocoa urn a row of twenty-four small white mugs were placed, next to a stack of round earthenware breakfast bowls, one for each boy.

Higher up the wooden box-type radio was positioned, with a little oval illuminated glass window in the center, containing a dial with a series of numbers. The movement of the dial's arrow always fascinated me much more than the dialogue, as it fluctuated side to side with the varying audio reception, frequently interrupted by static and not always very clear. On rare special occasions we were allowed to listen, although for some considerable time I did not really appreciate the significance of the verbal broadcasts but enjoyed the music.

On the other side, to the left of the doors set in an alcove diagonally across the corner, was a large, black iron stove, squatting on short, wrought iron legs with "cats paw" curled feet. The dual purpose was both heating the room in winter and keeping a large kettle or saucepan full of water hot on top.

The glowing fire was regularly fed with coke poured from a hand held scuttle, through a little round lid requiring a special tool to open it. The same two boys, who were allocated the task of cleaning the stove every morning, also kept it filled. Frequently a flimsy, wooden framed clothes-horse was arranged in front, draped with items of clothing hung out to dry.

One time Sisters clothes were placed too close and the sudden smell of scorched baggy bloomers brought the "Rat" to her feet in a panic, accompanied by smothered, half-hidden snickers from all those present.

Placed to one side a flat, open box was divided by a carrying handle into two sections, containing a tin of liquid grate polish and brushes used for polishing the dull black, cast iron until it virtually glistened. In the process hands became heavily stained by the liquid, leaving a strong pungent odor, difficult to remove, even after washing in a bar of abrasive carbolic soap supplied for all cleansing needs. A heavy, thick oilcloth apron with wide tapes was tied around the waist and looped over the head, to protect clothing. In cold weather this chore was one of the dirtiest, albeit the warmest, particularly when the front grill was open allowing the heat to escape into the room. As with all "before breakfast tasks", once the job was completed the sister was summoned to inspect the handiwork and "woe-betide" any boy if it was not up to her strict standards.

Directly in front of the stove, set against the far wall, the Sisters private dining table was positioned, a dark oak, round gate-leg table with four matching high-backed chairs, covered by flat floral seat cushions.

A vase of fresh flowers was always placed in the center of the table every morning before breakfast and removed after the last meal of the day. On special occasions, or on Sunday at tea-time, guests such as the Governor a neighboring Sister or a visiting Minister occupied one of the other seats, but normally just the two House Sisters sat there. The rare exception was when somebody's relative was visiting who may occasionally be invited to join them at their table, although my own mother or older sisters were never so privileged. At the far end of the room, extending the whole width of the wall, blank except for a large framed picture of Jesus, was one of two long wooden tables with low back-less benches placed either side, where six boys sat closely together facing six others on the opposite side.

Another similar table was positioned against the side wall, at right angles facing the window, allowing all twenty-four boys to be seated for meals at one time in full view of the Sisters. None of the dining tables were covered or decorated in any way and the edges of the thick wooden top had become scarred and splintered by frequent intentional misuse of blunt table knives, wielded by bored interns waiting patiently to be fed.

Older boys proudly pointed out to newcomers the interesting variety of signs and initials carved into the hard wood over many years. If caught in this act of vandalism naturally the punishment was swift and severe, involving six sharp whacks on a bare naked posterior with the black rubber slipper, nearly always executed in the boot room at the end of the hallway. Immediately following the offender would invariably be sent up to stay in the bedroom, leaving me to frequently wonder why during the day we were sent upstairs but relegated downstairs if caught misbehaving at night! If only we could somehow have stayed in limbo!

At the precise moment all boys' were seated for each meal, upon command we bowed our heads and recited the Methodist grace, led by the Sister.

"For what we are about to receive, may we be truly thankful"!

Under our breath at the conclusion and hopefully out of hearing, "long-timers" would mutter in unison; "Because we are not going to get anymore"!

Once the ritual was completed, a boy from each table was nominated to fill a white enameled jug with cocoa, from the tap at the bottom of the tall urn on the dresser, to be placed in the center of the table. After having been made in the kitchen early in the morning the liquid quickly became lukewarm, changing to an unappetizing grayish color, by the time morning tasks were completed and breakfast arrived. The cocoa powder was usually mixed with hot water without any additional milk or sugar, which was rationed during the War. Supposedly the concoction was already sweetened, but by the time it was poured into the mugs it was hardly fit to drink, and with highly chlorinated water being the only alternative the tepid off-color cocoa was preferable.

The Breakfast menu seldom varied from the usual bowl of thick porridge oats, with visible little black bits mixed in, which were never diagnosed, but we all harbored suspicions. The grey oatmeal was always made with plain hot water, although we were given the choice of adding salt to the thick lumpy mixture, a practice introduced by a former Scottish sister who had long since retired. Needless-to-say the condiment did not improve the flavor and not many boys took advantage of the privilege.

Thick, chunky slices of home-baked white bread were placed on a platter in the center of the table, sufficient only for one slice each boy. The moment grace was completed twelve hands reached simultaneously grabbing for the thickest piece, which was broken into pieces and dunked into the gray porridge before being devoured hungrily. Obviously the bigger the boy the larger his catch, particularly if he happened to be seated opposite the plate. The pecking order was established very early on and only changed when boys moved to different houses, left to return home, were shipped off abroad, or at an appropriate age and behavior, sent to a Methodist Theological College for training in the Ministry.

Rarely was anything proffered to spread on bread during the week, except the occasional dollop of fatty, beef dripping, left in the pan after the sisters Sunday dinner roast and poured into an earthenware bowl to congeal. Obviously the dark jelly-like substance at the base provided us with essential proteins and fats, which otherwise were sadly lacking in our frugal diets. Tea time at four on Sundays, before evening prayers was some-what of a special treat, when bread was cut a little thinner and spread sparingly with margarine, which became known as "cart grease". If Sister was in a very good mood or "The Rat" was away for some reason, we occasionally enjoyed a teaspoon full of homemade jam, doled out from the deep glass jam dish positioned on the privileged corner table. Upon arrival my designated position at the dining table was with my back towards the sisters table, never daring to turn around, but later having grown older it was permitted to sit against the far wall facing them. In this position it became possible to observe both sisters, plus any guests at the table, also the variety of gourmet foods they were privileged to savor.

Frequently we stared enviably at the meals they enjoyed, particularly at breakfast time, while desperately scoffing grubby little hunks of bread we had managed to grab. All manner of unaccustomed treats could be seen at different mealtimes, including crisp halves of buttered toast lined up in a silver rack, then delicately dipped into soft boiled, farm fresh brown eggs or spread with thick-cut orange marmalade. Mixed fruits from a crystal glass dish, were topped with cream spooned from a jug of fresh milk. Over twenty boys' stared wide eyed or drooled longingly, open mouthed at the sights, sniffing appreciatively at the aromas as the Sisters greedily consumed the appetizing morsels in full view, seemingly oblivious to our hungry gaze.

Occasionally, if personal good behavior warranted it on ones birthday, the lucky boy was called to humbly stand at the Head Sisters table and invited to choose a cake from the selection stacked on the layered, silver cake stand. It was, of course, considered friendly to pick the largest and share it with close pals. Once the announcement was made everyone sang "Happy Birthday" and watched enviously as the "Birthday Boy" rose to perform his role. At the same time cards and presents sent by relatives were handed out. Bad behavior within the Sister's recent memory, prior to your birthday, definitely eliminated the possibility of your name being called. There was always a boy who never received anything, although everyone shared in the excitement and anticipation of the fortunate one.

Weekends and holidays were the only times a midday meal was served at the home, because during the week the noon meal was provided at school. Local students from private homes always complained about the food but to "the urchins" it was infinitely more palatable than the slop we were accustomed to. Typical in-house menu items included cabbage boiled to a watery, dark gray consistency, clay colored sour lentils, sickening "Frog Spawn" tapioca or milk-less, unsweetened rice pudding that clung to the spoon.

If anything was left on the plate and not consumed at one sitting it was removed and marked with the offender's name, then re-presented the next day to be eaten cold before anything else. Naturally we developed devious ways of avoiding this vile practice, including wrapping unpalatable morsels in a filthy, ragged handkerchief or just stuffing them into a pocket to mix with the multitude of items already deposited. The stench of certain foods disposed of in this way lingered for days, if not conveniently flushed down the toilet or dropped into the long grass on the way to school, at the earliest opportunity. School meals, on the other hand, were always eaten with gusto and included any unwanted succulent item frequently pushed to one side by a local civilian picky diner. Wartime government rules concerning child menus were obviously more carefully observed by schools than other national institutions, both in the selection, preparation and presentation of foods, even during times of severe rationing. Before bedtime another cup of tepid cocoa was provided from the tall urn on the dresser and on rare occasions a plain oatmeal biscuit was also offered. It depended on the duty Sister and whether or not bad behavior warranted an "early to bed" punishment, usually directed immediately following teatime.

One morning at the age of about eight, while Sister Eileen was still in charge, I awoke feeling quite faint and sickly. Not wanting to be accused of slacking and managing, with some difficulty, to complete the designated morning task before breakfast, I took my usual place at the long dining table.

When the customary bowl of thick, lumpy oatmeal porridge was placed in front of me, I could only sit and stare at it unable to muster the appetite to eat. The longer the wait the more obnoxious it smelled, causing an increased sickening and frequent dizziness.

After a brief period when all the other boys had finished eating, "The Rat," who always kept a beady eye on us, rose from the sister's table crossed the floor and stood directly behind me.

"Why are you not eating boy! Is there something wrong with it?"

"No Sister." I replied weekly. "I don't feel well."

"Nonsense Boy, eat it up!"

Reluctantly picking up the spoon, lowering it into the bowl, I raised the loathsome concoction slowly toward my mouth but was incapable of actually opening my lips. At that instant the spoon was wrenched from my hand by long bony fingers and forced between my teeth, while her other hand firmly cupped my head backwards.

"Eat it Boy! Eat it!" She hissed through gritted teeth, while shoving my head violently down towards the wavering spoon.

Retching uncontrollably as the unsavory odor of the food sparked my senses, without warning the pit of my stomach erupted, ejecting hot bile straight into the bowl of porridge and swamping the table. Everything began to swirl and the last sounds heard before oblivion was "Eat it Boy! Eat it! Eat it!"

Awakening to the smell of antiseptic, in crisp clean hospital sheets, weak and feverish, discovering I had contracted a diseased liver condition known as Yellow Jaundice, which is characterized by the color of skin. A later diagnosis also confirmed intestinal tapeworms, not uncommon amongst young boys in the houses.

After spending a number of weeks in the hospital across The Green enjoying a special diet, my health slowly improved with treatment, aided by a variety of fresh fruits and other similarly unaccustomed delicacies. My Sisters and Brother who were actually allowed to visit me brought little gifts and most afternoons I lounged peacefully on the roof-top sunny veranda, watching other children play on the swings and seesaw in the grounds below.

Finally, fully recovered, released and unfortunately returned to Meriden House and Sister Eileen, who never mentioned the original breakfast episode, but my intense dislike for her and badly made oatmeal porridge continued indefinitely.

Another incident involving the Head Sister occurred in the bathroom, situated opposite the boot-room close to the back door. The bathroom was always a cold uninviting area, with rough, uneven gray flagstones on the floor and plain white tiles extending halfway up walls, painted a flaking pale, insipid green.

Below windows, set against the far wall, stood a row of six porcelain wash basins each fitted with two metal taps and a little rubber stopper on a thin metal chain used to plug the drain hole. The taps were marked hot and cold on top but the water flowing out from both was always at best tepid. Between the taps alongside each basin a rectangular block of pale yellow carbolic soap was always placed.

On a side wall rows of double-ended hooks were positioned within reach, that held towels and flannels by little white loops stitched onto one corner. Above each hook was a number corresponding with the one marked in black ink on the looped tape. Toothbrushes similarly numbered by white adhesive plaster, hung on smaller hooks through a little hole in the handle. As in the hall cloakroom each number signified individual owners.

Every morning during ablutions, each boy in turn, dipped his brush into a little flat tin containing a pink, gritty solution, titled "Gibbs Dentifrice Tooth Powder." The practice involved wetting the bristles first then dipping them into the powder to coat, before passing the tin down the line. By the time it reached the last boy the remaining mixture had become quite sloppy or slobbery, certainly not an appropriate blend to put in your mouth, so frequently this personal hygiene chore was avoided whenever unobserved. It is not difficult to imagine how numerous childhood illnesses were passed on in this manner.

Extending into the center of the room from behind the door, a deep, white enameled bathtub squatted on four curled iron feet, rusting through flaky, moldy paint. At the far end water pipes extended from the walls, looping over the edge of the bath attached to wide mouthed, chrome faded taps. Most of the metal covering had long since flaked off, leaving them a dull gray. On both the tub and washbasins the white enamel had also worn thin over the years, exposing streaks of dark metal and bright orange rust marks beneath the taps, caused by continual dripping. As hard as one tried, with all the "Elbow Grease," carbolic soap or gritty powder applied daily as a chore, neither could ever be completely removed, much to the obvious annoyance of the Head Sister!

Bath time was a regular Friday night ritual, taking place after tea before the bedtime cocoa, when large coke boilers were stoked, to hopefully get the water hot enough and last the length of time it took to bathe all boys in quick succession.

Early in the war the government had announced a directive that, to conserve energy and water, bathtubs should not be filled to more than a depth of five inches. The sisters religiously enforced this rule, at least in our bathtub, but needless to say the amount of water barely covered the essentials. In addition, to save water, it was not always changed after each boy but only drained after becoming cold or covered with thick grayish soap scum, dividing like slimy pond- weed as one entered.

Boys were lined up to wait, standing bare foot and naked, except for a thin threadbare towel clutched and draped around their scrawny, shivering bodies. Then, one at a time, as each bathed boy climbed out, another was beckoned to enter.

Older boys were usually allowed to bathe themselves, but frequently a sister wielding a stiff brush, doused in the gritty yellow soap, viciously scrubbed younger, grubbier unfortunates. Elbows and knees were prime targets but no area appearing slightly soiled escaped punishment. Two particular places subject to the closest scrutiny were the back and front of the neck where "tide marks" often appeared, woe-betide-you if they were spotted before having had a chance to wash alone. Whenever the hard bristled brush was used it left tender areas, remaining red and sore for days afterwards.

To protect her uniformed blue dress "The Rat" wore a full-length oilskin apron, hung from her neck and tied with tapes around her waist. There were times it was obviously necessary, particularly when the filthy water made the bottom and sides of the bath extremely slippery. Many a boy fell backwards on the way out causing almost a mini tidal wave, swamping the floor and frequently the Sisters feet, resulting in a swift swat across a naked backside with the back of a wooden handled brush.

Waiting in line a shoving contest often developed, while trying to determine whose turn coincided with the change in clean warm water. By the time older boys had finished it was always discolored and quite tepid, so frequently an attempt was made whenever the Sister was absent, to turn the hot tap on for a hopeful quick infusion.

Over the course of many years the unpleasant "Scum Bath" was frequently experienced but on one particular night, after being finally considered old enough to bathe myself, I was also at the head of the line when the water was changed.

Climbing into the tub as the sister coincidentally stepped out of the room for something, I proceeded to wallow in the warm water and soap myself all over with the soft flannel. It was very relaxing and pleasant after standing half naked on the cold wet floor and soon I was reveling in an enjoyable experience. At the time, early during the war at the age of only ten, apparently my body had begun to develop, although still very slightly built and quite skinny for my age, weighing only a little over fifty pounds. Regardless, I was quite fit and regularly participated in cross-country running and soccer, both at the secondary school and practically every free weekend on Orphanage grounds.

Whether it was the comfortable warm feeling or something to do with my maturing hormones was not known, but suddenly without warning "Little Willy" began to rise to the occasion, until it stuck out proudly erect! Other boys enviously waiting their turn could not help but notice my predicament. Pointing and bursting into loud hysterical laughter they excitedly danced around the tub, as I stood with my arms held proudly above my head whirling with gayest abandon, displaying my early signs of manhood for all to see.

At the height of the kafuffle the tall, dour-faced "Rat" unexpectedly returned and suddenly there was a noticeable hush.

"What are you doing boy?" She screamed, pointing at my lower extremities.

Looking down sheepishly at my rapidly shrinking appendage it was very obvious.

"You are a disgusting Boy! Put it away"!

How could it be put it away? There was nowhere to put it but protectively cup it in both hands? At that instant the wet, flat-backed scrubbing brush smacked down sharply onto my bare posterior with a resounding crack, instantly creating a rapidly enlarging reddening welt.

"Put it away," she repeated between gritted teeth, dealing me another stinging whack.

Then, without warning, suddenly dousing me with a bucket of cold water usually kept close by for cooling the hot bath, although seldom used and never before for this purpose.

"Act like a dog you'll be treated like a dog"! She hissed.

The combination of blows and cold water on my naked body certainly had the desired effect and the protuberance hurriedly shriveled back into its outer protective foreskin.

"Now get out and get dressed"! She commanded.

Shivering violently and slowly climbing out, watched by numerous smirking faces of those still in line, I thankfully wrapped myself once more in the threadbare towel. This one particular incident was destined to be retold and enlarged upon literally many times in the future, but at that precise moment I was grateful to escape her wrath, if only for a brief moment.

Incidentally the majority of boys in Meriden House were not circumcised, although one noticeable exception at a later date was my eventual new Jewish friend Paul, who came to the home after being evacuated from Austria early during the war. Needless to say, at his initial bath-time appearance the accompanying boys found his condition quite fascinating, much to his unfortunate personal embarrassment.

5

Church

After breakfast and before walking the few miles to school during the week, everyone attended compulsory morning prayers. Two by two, boys and girls separately, from each house, marched behind their particular head sister to the church. Inside they were ushered into long wooden pews to sit, before having to stand when the Methodist Minister, or the Governor, entered alone. On weekdays the full choir, who usually accompanied either of them, were not in attendance.

John Wesley (1703-1791) was the founder of Methodism in England. The National Children's Home had branches throughout the country staffed by Methodist Sisters and male clergy who preached his philosophy in their sermons, frequently quoting from his writings. John Bunyan's religious allegory, "Pilgrim's Progress" was another much quoted book we were regularly directed to read. I did once try during one of my lengthy periods of banishment but gave up before too many pages, finding it very difficult to understand. Generally, with few exceptions, the sermons were as boring and I frequently fell asleep, only to wake up suddenly as the congregation rose to sing or I was dealt a stinging finger flip behind one ear. One of the few exceptions was when a particular visiting clergy from a neighboring church attended, who seemed to have the knack of making his sermon more interesting, thereby holding the attention of the younger members of the congregation.

Sunday church service was also obligatory in the morning before dinner, while in the afternoon we attended bible classes for about an hour, before being allowed outside to play until the much anticipated teatime. Following tea everyone attended the evening service which was much less formal, without a lengthy sermon and with additional hymns, making it more enjoyable. Maurice and I always attempted to sit together when we were both in the same house and sang heartily, often grinning at each other until a sister spotted us. "Hymn singing was serious and not meant to be fun," we were frequently orally and physically reminded.

Church attendance also presented a rare opportunity to see our sisters, albeit at a distance, as both of them were, for a length of time, in the choir, although eventually when the range of my young singing voice was discovered, I also joined that privileged group. Before then, if lucky enough to be seated next to the aisle, it was possible to observe both my sisters attired in black cassocks and floppy, broad berets as they entered the nave and solemnly filed past my particular row, to take up positions either side of the altar.

The pulpit and lectern stood on a high platform in front of two rows of pews where choir members sat and I often tried to get my sisters attention, being careful not to catch the minister's eye, because having one of them notice me and smile back meant so much. Of course, if caught by the beady eyes of "the Rat," a sharp rap on the knuckles or a slap on the back of my head was administered. It amazed me how someone who behaved so horribly during the week could also become so pious in church, at times even managing the semblance of a smile if our eyes met during a hymn. Invariably being seated next to her, particularly as a new boy, I remember looking up in wonderment at the power and range of such a beautiful singing voice, which became so harsh and bitter under totally different circumstances.

Growing older, realization dawned as to how hypocritical it seemed when the minister ended his sermon or prayer with the words, "Lord, protect us from those who would do us harm," or "Protect these children in the name of God the Father Almighty"! Frequently, these persons of so-called good faith inflicted such unfair, cruel punishment on so many children in the home, in the name of God. Very few people known during my years spent in the home actually practiced what they preached, or professed to believe in, particularly the biblically prescribed act of forgiveness.

A regular custom on Sunday mornings before leaving the house was for all boys to line up, to be inspected in their "Sunday Clothes," to ensure a presentable appearance. At the same time each was given a single penny from a large bag of coins kept by the sisters, intended solely for the church collection. It was never actually discovered exactly where so many pennies came from, although on the annual Fete Day in the summer visitors threw coins into a large bag, strategically placed inside the archway entrance to the oval. So by depositing pennies into the collection bowl they became, supposedly, a kind of recycled donation.

On one fete occasion a friend and I once had the dubious responsibility of selling used postage stamps, piled in a whicker laundry basket, where visitors rummaged through a huge variety removed from envelopes throughout the year. In return philatelists donated a few coins for any of their chosen collectables.

At this particular time English coinage was twelve pence to the shilling and twenty shillings to the pound, equal to two hundred and forty pence. So with each boy receiving one penny, approximately two shillings a week was contributed from each house. The House Sisters, on the other hand, extravagantly dropped a minimum of sixpence or sometimes even a shilling as their own individual offering. After observing this it later crossed my mind they may be attempting a little pre-heaven lobbying.

After the sermon and during the final hymn, two ushers would pass a wooden bowl for the congregation to deposit their donation. Moving slowly down the aisle from the front pew to the last at the rear of the church, the bowls were collected and taken forward to the impressively robed figure waiting in front of the altar. With great ceremony the minister would raise them above his head, before stacking the bowls on the altar, muttering a soft command, "Let us pray," as we all knelt for the final benediction. The collection, we were often informed, was to be donated to "needy children separated by the war." My feelings were that our individual needs were probably just as great as anyone else's, if not greater. The grand finale came as the organist loudly thumped out a stirring patriotic tune, whereupon everyone filed out of the church row by row, to be mustered back into pairs for the short walk around the perimeter of the oval to their respective houses.

The Sunday dinner following the church service was always eagerly anticipated as the better meal of the week, because we were actually served the semblance of a dessert, although the usual inedible first course, still frequently included hard, black-eyed potatoes and over boiled, insipid cabbage. Deserts were certainly not gourmet either, consisting mainly of powdered milk tapioca (known as "frogs-spawn"), semolina, or plain rice. On rare Sundays, if one's behavior in church warranted it, or the sister had enjoyed the service, we were given a spoonful of jam or treacle to sweeten the pudding, making the concoction at least palatable, if not calorific.

After the sumptuous Sunday repast, if the weather was fine, we were taken for a customary walk in the nearby park, presumably to work off the extra energy gained. Frequently during these outings local boys harassed us, shouting foul suggestions questioning our parentage. Many times a number of us boys were involved in confrontations with local gangs, who delighted in antagonizing or taunting us as orphans, in the mistaken belief that none of us had parents. Even if we managed to convince them otherwise, we were branded as illegitimate anyway. Sister Eileen accompanying us on the walk strode ahead with head held high, seemingly oblivious to the taunts, commanding us to "ignore the urchins." We always obeyed, until allowed out without supervision, when we invariably retaliated by squaring off in a pitched battle atop a deep clay quarry close by the town of Kingstanding. The first group to arrive at the site occupied the high ground but late arrivals, lower in the pit, frequently retreated from a barrage of stones hurled from above. Unfortunately, it was once my predicament to be caught with a couple of friends and suffer a rock pelting, which inflicted wounds and scars on the back of my head visible to this day.

There were times, obviously, when my demeanor was not as angelic as perhaps it should have been, and by admission this enables me to confess my sins, although at the time of minor indiscretions my boyish actions were never considered particularly sinful or irreverent. For seemingly endless Sundays dutifully placing my penny in the collection bowl and passing it on to the next person, I never considered doing anything else. Growing older, however, I discovered not all boys were as pious as at first thought and it didn't take long to realize why they were often able to spend more money at the Tuck Shop than others. Attending a group get-together one day in the playground lavatory block, one of the boys proudly described how he had avoided placing his coin in the plate for some considerable time. Producing a penny he proceeded to demonstrate his "sleight of hand" prowess, by deftly palming the coin while appearing to drop it with the other hand. Needless to say we all practiced fervently for the next six days, desperate for the next Sabbath to arrive to try out and hopefully benefit from our newly acquired skill.

Listening to the usual boring sermon, growing nervous with anticipation and clutching the coin in my sweaty palm, I turned it over and over in my pocket. Fortunately my seat was not close to the sister but positioned in front and a couple of spaces away, considered safe.

During the singing of the final hymn, watching nervously as the collection plate was brought closer and finally handed to the boy at the end of the first row it was slowly passed person to person down to me. At the time noticeably, there were quite a few coins in the plate, not just pennies. Anything larger than a sixpence or shilling, such as a half-a-crown, usually meant there were outside visitors in the front pew and there were rumors of a boy who once attempted to remove such a coin, without success and with dire consequences.

Taking hold of the plate with my left hand, turning towards the next boy and at the same time placing my right hand over the top I pretended to drop the coin as rehearsed. Adroitly palming the penny, or so I thought, I went to pass the plate on still singing and feeling very cocky, thinking; "Boy will I have a tale to tell"! Unfortunately forgetting how tall "the Rat" was and how far her beady little eyes could see over our heads.

Suddenly, without warning, my ear was seized in the middle of a musical stanza, causing an involuntary emission of a high-pitched, tuneless squeal. A bony grip twisted my head backward to look into the mean face of Sister Eileen, as she stretched an elongated arm across the row, no smile, lips drawn tight, eyes half closed. "Put it on the plate!" she rasped, as her other arm firmly held the wrist of the boy patiently waiting next to me. Continuing to hold the collection plate I obediently dropped the penny to clink in with the other coins and her grip was released. Then as if nothing had happened, without further glance or pause, the sister resumed her singing of the last verse oblivious to my nervous gaze.

There was no doubting the upcoming consequences after committing such a "sacrilegious act" as trying to withhold an offering, even though I had considered my needs greater. Assuredly I was later denied Sunday dinner and once again endured the dreaded "Black Slipper," before being sent up to stay in the bedroom for the remainder of the afternoon.

Missing the best meal of the week was bad enough and six whacks of the slipper were endured, but having to spend a whole Sunday afternoon alone in the bedroom when friends were outside playing, was considered a worst punishment and one unfortunately frequently administered during my years in the home.

The Harvest Festival Service held every autumn had always fascinated me, when the front of the church was gaily decorated with a huge variety of fruits, flowers and vegetables. Along the edge of the raised platform in front of the lectern and pulpit, a row of highly polished fruits and vegetables were interspersed with sheaves of yellow wheat, carefully laid out. Every house contributed jars of homemade preserves, fruits bottled by the sisters or wonderful baked breads including succulent pastries, never before seen let alone sampled. The farmer delivered the sheaves of wheat, vegetables and fruits the day before the service, accompanied by the head gardener who provided a huge display of colorful potted plants and flowers. The Baker, Mister Salt, displayed a selection of multi-shaped, crusty golden brown loaves adorned with an incredibly artistic wheat-sheaf pattern baked on top. Marveling enviously at the display and drooling uncontrollably throughout the service, particularly after becoming a member of the choir positioned in such close proximity, the aroma activated my taste buds making singing extremely difficult.

On one occasion, privileged to be one of a small number chosen to help carry and position the items in front, under supervision, the temptation to sample from the wonderful selection became overpowering and I admit to eventually succumbing to subterfuge when the adult supervisor left briefly. A huge basket of fresh, rosy red apples and delicious yellow pears was centered in front of the altar, flanked by long sheaves of maize and two giant green marrows. The sight and scent was just too much to bear and in an instant I reached out and grabbed one of the pears, stuffing it with some difficulty into my short trouser pocket unseen, or so I thought. Unfortunately after we had finished the display I discovered my indiscretion had not gone completely unnoticed. Outside the church, on the way back to the house, one of the older boys who had obviously noticed the dastardly act, demanded I produce it and share or else! Naturally I did as commanded, not wishing a confrontation, but even half a pear was the most succulent fruit I had tasted at the time.

I felt certain that if there were a God he would surely forgive a hungry boy for such an opportunistic act. During the actual Harvest Festival Service that followed there was certainly something to sing about and I really was, for once, truly grateful for what I had received, although I couldn't help notice the vacant space in the basket where the plump, ripe pear had once been.

Upon contemplation later in life, I realized the necessity to steal food in particular was an unfortunate skill developed at a very early age. Cheating and deliberately lying were lessons well learnt over the years, mainly to avoid severe self or group punishment, although often administered for escapades which perhaps now, in this modern era, are considered normal childish behavior? Certainly preachers and sisters were totally unaware of the negative affect their disciplinary actions, applied so stringently in the name of religion, had on such young, innocent minds. In my opinion and those of many other former orphans the lesson, "The Lord will provide," somehow never materialized. Church teachings taught us how we were expected to behave but those empowered with everyday indoctrination unwittingly forced us how to choose to behave, in order to overcome so many disadvantages.

One benefit resulting from church attendance came when I finally joined the choir and met Sister Fanny from the nursery school once again, who still conducted the weekly choir practices in the long wooden hut behind the girl's houses. This dedicated sister was one of a few people who perhaps may have converted me and definitely encouraged me to sing well enough to become a soloist in church, even performing at public concerts and actually enjoying the experience. As a member of the choir, I at least managed to be away from the strict control of Sister Eileen in the pews but even that privilege was put at risk once, when the male choirmaster caught me in the act of flicking paper pellets at younger choirgirls. Pages torn from the back of the hymn book were chewed and rolled into little round pellets, then flicked toward the back of the person's head in front. Unfortunately my aim was not always true and a stray pellet once landed within his sight, resulting, fortunately, only in a verbal warning that, "Any reoccurrence would result in immediate dismissal". Needless to say this was a deterrent for continuing the practice, plus not wishing to prejudice one of the few opportunities to see my sisters and thankful that my indiscretion was not reported further.

At the conclusion of the church services and Sunday dinner, if good behavior warranted it, we were generally encouraged outside to play in the afternoon. If Head Sister had not arranged to take us on walks to the park, or around local housing estates, each of us either individually or in a group would find our own particular form of amusement. Some played or just sat together on The Green Oval, while others utilized the swings and roundabouts in the playground next to the hospital.

Certain boys, of course, often found more adventurous escapades, which invariably got one or more into trouble. Climbing trees, fantasizing in an old wrecked motorcar in the lower play area, or investigating forbidden buildings were a few of the most popular pranks. Boredom contributed in great part to our search for adventure and left to our own devices or let loose to run, it was inevitable we resorted to mischief. Seldom, on Sundays, did we receive any practical guidance or encouragement from the sisters to participate, individually or collectively, in games or hobbies of educational benefit other than nature walks in the park or religious studies.

One of the forbidden areas both my brother and I, at different times, found exciting and at times frightening, was the bell tower of the church overlooking The Oval. On one wet dreary day having taken shelter in the back entrance to the church, I discovered a previously unnoticed door. Curiosity caused me to try the huge black, wrought iron latch that opened the thick wooden door, exposing a narrow staircase ascending the center of the tower. With multiple thoughts running through my mind I took tentative, hesitating steps upward, simultaneously brushing away the dusty cobwebs from my face. Nearing the top, stairs opened onto a small wooden platform and sunlight came through lead-framed windows surrounding the giant centered clock face. Loud rhythmic ticking coincided with the visible regular movement of the long, pointed second hand. High above in the belfry an enormous bell hung silent, from long, dangling, thick ropes almost within reach. Standing on tiptoe straining to my full height of about four feet, I peered out at the vast green oval spreading below. There was a clear view of everything, children playing and the hospital on the far side, even the farm buildings and beyond to the perimeter of The Orphanage grounds and privately owned suburban homes. It was a panoramic sight yet to behold, instantly becoming master of all I surveyed.

Suddenly, without warning, the sound of someone climbing the stairs made me look around desperately for a place to hide in the tiny space. Locating a dark cubbyhole behind the solid sloping beams supporting the bell frame, I managed to hastily crawl in and crouch down, peering between the spider webs and dusty wooden joints.

"If caught up here I'm in a lot of trouble," I thought.

The footfalls came closer and into view baggy turned up trousers, drooping below the knee, creasing onto grubby black, lace up boots. Reaching the top of the platform the heels lifted, as the man stretched onto his toes and the bell began to ring. Loud, deafening tolls forced me to place my hands hurriedly over my ears and huddle onto bent knees. Four times it rang, before thankfully stopping, as my ears continued to echo the sound. The boots turned and walked away to descend the stairs through the narrow exit, while nervously watching as the remainder of the body and head came into view, helping me recognize him as one of the senior male members of the choir who presumably also volunteered as the bell ringer. Fortunately he was looking down the steps as he disappeared from sight, failing to notice me huddling in the dark, spidery shadows.

Waiting, holding my breath until the lower door closed and carefully stepping back onto the platform I peered out of the window, to see him walking briskly back along the pathway away from the church. High above me, even from behind, the pointed hands did indeed show four o'clock, as I slowly made my way back down the staircase and out through the heavy door into the daylight, thankful to have eluded discovery and the inevitable punishment, at least one more time.

Frequently, on other summer afternoons, I would make my way down to the hay meadows, behind the hospital, where the farm horses grazed. If they were not turned out it was pleasurable to lie back in the long grasses completely alone and hidden, or so I thought, among the abundance of wild flowers. It was a peaceful place where one forgot worries and soaked up the warmth of the sun, oblivious to the rest of the world. The only sounds to disturb the silence were the drone of an occasional single prop airplane engine, high in the cloudless, clear blue sky or the humming of busy honey bees and insects.

One balmy Sunday after church when nearly twelve, my regular reverie was abruptly interrupted as I rested with my arms folded above my head, chewing a natural, prolific herb known locally as "vinegar leaves," while watching a hawk lazily gliding overhead, obviously on the lookout for field mice.

"Hello!" an unexpected musical female voice declared. "Who are you?"

Looking up blinking against the sunlight, filtering through long, shimmering, golden hair, framing a shadowy, silhouetted face, I rolled over and sat up to observe a vision of unforgettable childlike beauty.

Dressed in a knee-length, flared, pretty pink frock with a white lace collar and matching broad sash around her waist, she stood above me. Below the hem, at the knees, white silken stockings extended down slim legs and ankles to dainty, black patent leather shoes, adorned with shiny silver buckles. Gaping in wonderment, dumbfounded, never having seen anyone so lovely up until that time. No other known girl from any of the houses had ever dressed so prettily. Even on Sundays when they normally wore starched, light blue or green gingham dress- es, and definitely not the usual dark blue gym slip uniform ordered for school with navy knickers and plain black stockings. Neither of which ever did anything to arouse the boyish hormonal instincts I was now suddenly experiencing.

"Can't you speak? Don't you have a name?" came the question in a golden toned voice.

"Of course I do," stammering, open-mouthed, slowly rising to my knees.

The remainder of our conversation is a vague memory, as we sat to- gether among the wild grasses and flowers for what seemed an eternity talking, while the beautiful vision braided daisies and buttercups into a chain, laughingly draping them around my neck. Once, as she leant forward I hesitatingly kissed her on the cheek and she smiled without speaking. True love had struck for the very first time.

All too soon, two other senior girls, recognized as members of the choir, came running down the slope calling to her and she stood to wave back.

"I have to go."

"Will I see you again?" I queried hopefully.

"Maybe," she replied, smiling.

Unfortunately I never did but I still remember that first brief moment of ecstasy in my otherwise miserable world. Some time later, my sister Audrey, who frequently used to baby sit for the Governor, informed me that the young girl was probably his niece who had been visiting and attended the morning church service. For many Sundays I returned to the spot in the meadow after our meeting, but never saw her again either there or in church, and often wondered if she remembered the short, skinny shy boy in the meadow.

Other Sunday afternoons were later spent wandering down the narrow, high-banked lane towards the farm, where boys frequently met girls walking or sitting on the steep, grass covered verges to stop and talk or flirt. Normally we were discouraged from fraternizing with girls, even a sidelong glance incurred a swift hand-scuff to the head from a staff sister, but on rare occasions we were far enough away from the home grounds to be safe. It was rare for any member of staff to venture far away from their customary stroll around the grass oval in front of the church or hospital. Just being alone with prettily-dressed girls created a whole new experience and sitting close, observing form and movement, listening to silly girlish chatter excited boyhood instincts seldom experienced. During the remaining summers every available Sunday found me wandering down the lane hoping to find new girl-friends, eventually one in particular I came to know very well.

One particular girl I grew to love in a different more sisterly manner was Ruth, who kind of adopted me in a paternal way after Audrey and Pauline had left The Orphanage to return home. Our friendship grew until, after feeling I could confide in her, we often met when she cycled across to the main Orphanage from the senior girls' house on Chester Road, just outside the grounds. Our meetings were always eagerly anticipated and although a few years older, our friendship continued until I was almost thirteen, when an unexpected tragedy occurred, affecting me for a considerable time.

Practically every day after school when I was allowed out, Ruth, who was quite tall and slim with light brown, short, bobbed hair, often sat with me on a bench near the playing fields and read, told stories or just talked.

She would question me about school and the day-to-day activities in the house and I always told her everything that had happened because she was such a sympathetic listener, ready with words of advice and often a special sweet treat. As a senior girl Ruth enjoyed certain privileges, including earning extra spending money, which I often benefited from, together with an understanding and kindness seldom received from anyone else.

One day, leaving Meridan House to walk across the playing fields by the back gate, where we usually met, a boy from another house came frantically running up to me. "There's been an accident outside on the road!" he declared breathlessly, "They've sent for the ambulance, I think it's your girlfriend!" Certain boys often teased me about our relationship, which had become common knowledge.

Fearing the worst I ran desperately out of the gate onto the pavement at the edge of the road, where a small crowd of people had gathered by a parked single-decker, "Midland Red" bus. Trapped beneath the nearest, huge front wheel lay a crumpled bicycle I recognized, all twisted and mangled. To one side, on the concrete pavement, a familiar lone figure lay still sprawled on her back, with the uniformed, female Bus Conductor leaning over her. Ruth was obviously in a great deal of pain, it showed on her face normally so gentle and beautiful, now agonized and wet with tears flowing over her pale cheeks. Following the length of her arm, downward to her legs, the reason for her anguish and the concern of those surrounding her was obvious and an unforgettable sight. Her right ankle was crushed and bloody, twisted to one side in an unnatural, unaccustomed position. Looking away and then back to her sad face our eyes met, as she made a desperate attempt to smile reassuringly at my obvious shocked expression. Utterly devastated my eyes filled with uncontrollable tears. When the ambulance finally arrived attendants lifted her gently onto a stretcher, as I tearfully watched they slid it into the vehicle and the doors closed, before slowly moving off. The hysterical shrill sound of the large silver bell on the front of the ambulance, carrying my friend away, gradually faded far into the distance.

Later, from an observer, it was disclosed Ruth had been riding along the edge of the pavement towards the back entrance, possibly to meet me, when somehow the front wheel of the bicycle slipped sideways off the curb into the gutter, under the wheel of the closely following bus.

We were never able to enjoy our meetings again and much later I was informed that the most elegant Ruth I once knew, eventually returned to the home wearing an ugly iron leg brace and a high-blocked, black lace-up boot. Thankfully I never saw her in that condition, but sadly was never to meet my beautiful, sympathetic friend again before eventually leaving the Children's Home.

6

The War

The Second World War, beginning in September 1939 and lasting until August 1945, was spent languishing and slowly maturing between the ages of seven and thirteen in The Orphanage. The War didn't affect us very much individually, seeming to waft over the airwaves except on rare occasions. Although it certainly had the effect of bringing people closer together and softening, or even changing the attitude of a few of those who looked after us. There sometimes appeared to be more concern for our welfare by particular individuals with friends or family members who had been "called up", or were involved in the "war effort". However, problems brought about by the war certainly did not appear to change the attitude of the Head Sister Eileen towards her young charges.

About this time rumors began to circulate that "The Rat" was leaving, causing great excitement among all boys culminating in the announcement by the governor, at morning prayers, explaining that Sister Eileen was actually leaving for Australia. Quite probably to accompany some of the poor unfortunates who were being shipped to that "Outpost of the Empire?" Although at the time we were totally unaware of the government's despicable program for homeless and orphaned children, removed from bombed-out neighborhoods. The day of departure, when the Head Sister walked out the front door away from the house, is vividly recalled. My brother and I, together with a group of boys, stood quietly chanting in unison; "Rats, Rats we have to get rid of the rats", a tuneless dirge we had frequently sung together, but never within earshot for risk of suffering terrible repercussions.

Sister Eileen strode up the pathway leading to the main offices clutching a small suitcase, head up seemingly completely oblivious to the crescendo of abuse following her, which increased in volume as she moved further away. It was the last we ever saw of her but with knowledge gained later, I hated to think of how many more minors in a far off land also suffered from her self imposed, strict religious discipline and forms of punishment in the future.

Next day her replacement arrived and all boys were lined up to meet the new Head Sister in the front hallway by Sister Eva, whom we had all hoped would now hold that position. Sister Nellie Hunter hailed from Manchester with a very distinct northern accent and, unlike the tall slim stature of Sister Eileen, was considerably shorter and rather stout. Once dark, graying hair was bobbed short above her shoulders and held back at the temples with long, bronze colored metal grips. A short plumpish nose was centered between podgy red cheeks and deep-set icy blue, penetrating eyes peered from beneath heavy eyelids. We were soon to learn, depending on her mood, that her eyes could either soften and sparkle when pleased, or harden with an intimidating, fixed stare when angry. What really caught one's attention and always fascinated me was a bulbous, brown, hairy mole situated on the right side of her chin just below the lower lip. Her appearance early on earned her the nickname of "Billy Bunter," who was a pudgy, obnoxious schoolboy character, featured in a popular boy's cartoon comic of the period. At first her nature appeared more kindly than her predecessor, but before very long opinions changed drastically.

Another early absentee from his administrative duties early in the war was the Governor, Mr. Jacka, who was a reserve officer in The Royal Air Force. Once again an announcement was made from the pulpit, at morning prayers, that he had been "Called Up" to active service. The Assistant Governor, Mr. Roycroft, took over duties during his absence and although we saw Mr. Jacka a number of times in the future, resplendent in uniform and colorful chest ribbons, whilst presumably on leave, he never returned as Governor after the war. Maybe it was my youthful age during his short term but I always thought of him as a kindly man, his appearance and stature somewhat similar to the famous French General Charles De Gaulle.

It was inevitable that many more children, particularly those from European countries invaded by the Nazi's, would eventually arrive at the home. One who came to Meriden was a Jewish boy whose family had escaped from Vienna, named Paul David, who for his age was quite tall with cropped blonde hair and bright blue eyes. Unfortunately, he also possessed a rather prominent nose, which of course the boys made fun of behind his back. The ridicule was wasted, however, because he couldn't understand a word of English when he first arrived.

Austria had allied with the Germans before the outbreak of war and many Jewish families were forced to leave due to Nazi extermination plans. Paul's mother, an elegant, well dressed lady in an expensive looking fur collared coat and matching hat, brought him to the house, where I was directed to show him around by Sister Nellie. Later he became one of my closest friends and we spent many hours together sitting on the playroom floor, or out on the front oval, while he tried to learn English. My own acquired Midlands or "Brummy" accent obviously made it even more difficult for him to understand, but hopefully he eventually lost it as he grew up and moved out into the world. I often wondered what became of him and whether he eventually returned to live in Austria after the war. Coincidentally, later in life during my military career, three years were spent posted to Austria during the four power occupation, where many of the happiest times of my life were enjoyed in that beautiful country.

Very early on things began to happen making us very aware of what the war really meant. Workmen came to each house and stuck sticky tapes diagonally across all the windows, carefully explaining it helped prevent the glass shattering from an explosion. Other houses had wooden shutters installed outside the windows to protect the glass and black curtains were hung and drawn tightly closed at sunset, to prevent any light from showing outside. Volunteer Wardens also walked the grounds after sunset and at night to check for any chinks of light showing, while streetlights were hooded above the dome to deflect the light down, or actually turned off during an air raid. Similarly, all motor vehicles headlights were half covered with paint or little metal masks, giving the appearance of a giant beetles eyelids.

Later, numerous cars carried huge canvas "gas bags" on roof racks, filled with a propane gas to replace petrol, which was strictly rationed except for essential vehicles and caused as a result of the sinking of so many oil tankers by German "U Boats". Petrol rationing did not affect us individually but later, other essentials like butter, cheese, sugar and particularly chocolates and sweets were severely restricted, although these made little difference to our normal daily lives, because we never enjoyed many of those treats anyway even before rationing. Coupon books were issued for every child in the home, but we seldom ever actually saw them, because they were retained by the head sister together with any money sent to us.

Current behavior always determined when and how much we eventually received, while all mail was opened before we received it and even letters written home were handed in to be "censured," before being mailed.

Saturday was supposed to be "Pocket Money Day", when every boy who had behaved correctly all week received three pence spending money, together with the appropriate ration coupons. Even the slightest infringement of rules that may have annoyed the Head Sister during the week would mean the loss of these privileges. Needless to say I was often penniless, as were a number of boys during my period of stay, for various reasons. Anyone who was denied this privilege was forced to scrounge from, so-called "sister's pets," or "persuade" them to share, by fair means or foul. On the rare occasions I qualified, a hurried trip was made out the back gate across the Chester Road to the "Tuck Shop" for sweets, or a pennyworth of broken biscuits from a large wooden display barrel situated in the front doorway. Mixed, broken biscuits did more to temporally satisfy constant hunger pangs than boiled sweets, which required coupons. I am now convinced that the lack of sugar in my early diet did much to ensure the good condition of my teeth for so many years, until an unfortunate accident on a horse much later in life broke my jaw and wrecked most of them.

With the introduction of rationing, coin machines which dispensed chocolate bars became obsolete and were either taken away for scrap to help the war effort, or just left to rust as reminders of more happy days. Similarly, on grocer's shelves, brightly colored packages with trade names and fancy slogans disappeared, replaced with dull colored cardboard boxes merely titled in black. Washing Powder, Flour, Sugar, etc; all in the same plain lettering and dull cartons, it was very depressing! Food at the dining tables did not alter very much either, as we seldom were given any special treats anyway. The menu remained very basic, repetitive and most of the time almost inedible, providing very little of what growing, virile boys needed. By the time "Victory in Europe" was declared in 1945, at the age of thirteen, my height was only four feet six inches, weighing less than seventy-five pounds, in spite of a few risky night-time pantry plunders.

Another significant event, happening very early during the war, was the sudden removal of iron railings forming the perimeter fence surrounding The Orphanage. Without warning one day, we watched in amazement as workmen removed the high ornately figured fence from the solid concrete foundations. Long oxyacetylene flame cutters, attached by a rubber hose to a tank on the back of a lorry, were used to slice the metal into pieces, then thrown up and stacked carefully at the side of the road in huge bundles, leaving only small, sharp stumps protruding above the base on the ground. We were informed the precious metal was to be used to make guns and ammunition in local small arms factories for the "War Effort". However, stacks of old garden railings were left rusting in many nearby suburban streets long after hostilities had ended. Non-the-less, for a short while we thankfully enjoyed an unaccustomed freedom of exit and entrance, until another group of workmen finally replaced the old iron fence with wooden posts and thick wire mesh.

In May of 1940, Winston Churchill at the age of sixty-five years, succeeded Neville Chamberlain as Prime Minister and from that time on things seemed to worsen, as the real meaning of war was suddenly made clear to us. Bombing raids in the Midlands increased and on the night of the fourteenth of November, coincidentally my brother's birthday, the German "Luftwaffe" unleashed the most catastrophic bombing of the war on the City of Coventry. Over five hundred airplanes attacked and much of the city center was destroyed, including the famous cathedral, together with small-arms munitions factories and the BSA Motorcycle factory which employed many local workers, including women. The overnight devastation killed 554 civilians and wounded 865, while between the eighteenth and thirtieth of November, the city of Birmingham was also bombed numerous times. Every raid brought the sound of wailing sirens echoing through the dark foggy streets, followed by the deep drone of hundreds of enemy bombers passing overhead as we sat huddled, shivering in the damp, vermin infested underground bomb shelters.

Air Raid Shelters had been built underground earlier, on an open area behind each of the boy's houses, facing the football and sports fields. Huge mounds of earth enveloped corrugated iron roofs arching over puddle-ridden concrete floors, with slatted, wooden pallet walkways extending down the center.

On either side, a low wooden bench, running the full length of the cramped, tube-like building, gave a step up to long rows of narrow shelf-type bunks. Outside at one end, half hidden by long grass, thick metal doors were always kept locked until air raid sirens sounded, then opened by a man wearing a rounded, white-painted metal hat with a large black W on the front, as boys entered, two by two. The letter identified him as the Air Raid Warden, responsible for making sure everyone was safely under cover. It was usually members of the male staff, gardeners, farmhands, etc, who volunteered for this nightly duty on the grounds, whereas outside, in the surrounding town, it was the local police responsibility or more elderly members of the Home Guard. As the war progressed, every able- bodied person whether male or female, young or old, was called upon to help in the "war effort" in one way or another.

Underground air-raid shelters were used frequently during the winter of 1940, throughout England, when bombing raids intensified. One British Broadcasting Companies Home Service announced that over 1700 German aircraft had been shot down, with only 915 British fighter planes lost. Occasionally we were allowed to listen to the news broadcasts, on the radio in the Dining Hall, when we would literally try to keep score. Fortunately, it was frequently my advantage to listen to the Sisters sitting room radio, from my relegated punishment position, beneath the playroom bench. This enabled me to later inform and enlighten my friends, who otherwise may have been a little out of touch with current war news.

On one occasion with Maurice we sneaked out of the house, totally forbidden, to watch the bombers silhouetted against the night sky overhead. A squadron of huge dark-winged shadows, in formation, flew low enough for us to observe the black crosses on the wings and sides. Even during the day, on the way to school, we also watched "Dog Fights" between The Royal Air Force Spitfire and Hurricane defenders, against the slower German Messerschmitt and Dornier attackers.

The winter of 1940, reported by the BBC, was one of the worst in living memory, with long periods of bitter cold weather and heavy snowfalls, making the frequently extended periods in the cold, damp shelters even more miserable.

On one such night, we awoke to the sound of wailing sirens, as Sister Nellie came bustling up stairs commanding us to bring a blanket and gather in the downstairs hallway. After lining up in pairs, we were led out through the back door across to the shadowy shelters. On the way, looking up, hundreds of droning aircraft could be seen silhouetted, flying overhead, as we scuttled down into the damp, dark, cave-like interior.

Scrambling from the low bench onto the narrow wooden bunks above, we crouched side-by-side wrapped in thin red blankets, as anti aircraft guns fired off from positions in emplacements, built during the previous summer in the nearby park. Short crashes of gunfire were interspersed by a much louder, earth-shaking crunch that vibrated throughout the hollow shelter, whenever a bomb exploded. As the war progressed we experienced the more frightening "Buzz Bombs" or V2 Rockets, equipped with an engine which suddenly ceased before plunging to the ground. Literally, we held our breath between engine cut out and the explosion, not daring to inhale until the sudden anticipated violent impact nearby.

Inevitably someone started to cry as the small bulkhead lights, set in little protective metal frames, flickered and dimmed momentarily. I recalled my Grandmother saying, "The more you cry the less you pee," without really appreciating the connection at the time.

Once, in a brief period of quiet, the door suddenly opened and a figure in a dark raincoat and a familiar Wardens' tin hat entered, carrying a stack of flat metal baking trays balanced precariously in his arms. Mister Salt, the Baker, which was actually his real name and occupation; although we often acquainted him with the popular card game of the time called "Snap"; had apparently prepared for this emergency earlier in the day by baking a special batch of Fig Biscuits. He proceeded to hand out one to each boy in turn, walking slowly along the narrow center aisle, balancing precariously on the frail wooden pallets covering the damp concrete floor.

"It will be all over soon, don't worry, here you are" he exclaimed to each boy in turn with a cheery smile. Then he retreated outside once more, presumably to move on to the next shelter. The fruity biscuits tasted so good and were such an unaccustomed wholesome treat, they almost made us forget there was an air raid going on!

After one particular raid's "all clear," we discovered a stray bomb had almost struck The Greenhouse in the gardens, landing close by in a vegetable patch and shattering all the glass. German bombers were in the habit of jettisoning any bombs left over indiscriminately in the countryside, after targeting major cities, making the efforts of Mister Salt even more courageous, considering The Greenhouses were next door to his bakery!

Later in the war, following a rumored affair, he married Sister Mildred from Shaftsbury House, where my sister Pauline had stayed, eventually raising a son born in their cottage home at The Orphanage. Both Mister Salt and the Farmer, Mister Hall, were possibly the only two men known to me who actually behaved in a paternal or fatherly manner to most of the boys. Both men always demanded hard work and strict obedience, whilst displaying noticeable concern for our welfare and frequently showing individually unaccustomed kindnesses. Future air raids created land craters in nearby fields, where we were often able to pick up pieces of shrapnel, which became prized possessions, kept for bargain swapping later. Apparently, one discarded bomb actually landed on the farm buildings, killing two of my heavy workhorse friends in the lower meadows, during earlier more peaceful, humdrum summer days.

At the nearby local school we practiced air raid drills, crouching under little wooden desks when the sirens sounded warnings, often wondering how much protection the little wooden desks would provide, if an actual hit was made on the building. Thankfully one never was, although I frequently almost willed an air raid, particularly in the middle of a despised arithmetic lesson, for which at the time I failed to understand the logic. Every other subject was enjoyable, especially English and History which became my favorites. The "Boldmere Secondary Modern School" was located a few miles away from The Orphanage in the town of Sutton Coldfield, famous after the war for having erected one of the first ever television towers. Every weekday we walked in pairs out the back gate onto Jockey Road, where we soon separated with a particular friend to take a well known short cut through side streets, past a number of middle class private residences. Usually pairing up with my friend Johnny Butterworth as he was older and had been at the home longer, consequently knew all kinds of little tricks and dodges. Many of which were learnt fast and beneficial in a variety of ways well into the future, although not always to my distinct individual advantage.

By the time we had begun making our way to school, the Milkman, atop his horse drawn wagon had completed delivery rounds, depositing a requested number of silver or gold-topped bottles of milk on the front doorstep of certain private residences. Some of the occupants collected their milk early, others for whatever reason did not, which later proved to our advantage. After enduring the usual pitiful plate of watered down, sugarless porridge and hunk of plain bread, spread with greasy beef dripping, for breakfast, our systems were naturally very receptive to a heavy dose of rich protein to get us through the long school day. The temptation to pilfer was, therefore, often too much and we naturally frequently succumbed to the Devils prompting.

While one boy kept watch for a pedestrian passerby, or a face at the window, the other swiftly entered the gate and streaked up the garden path to the front door. Thankfully most residents who owned dogs kept them in back fenced gardens, or indoors if away at work, to protect delivering trades-people. Snatching a full bottle from the step and stuffing it beneath one's coat, to make a swift exit became an acquired art, which improved with practice and reaped rich rewards. As we became accomplished it became possible to even differentiate between a gold top, which was full cream, or the silver which was not, or even between a half-pint and a full pint bottle. After making a hundred-yard dash out to the street in record time we hid behind a suitable hedge or fence, to hastily gulp down the contents and dispose of the incriminating evidence. Only once were we almost caught by an observant or nosey neighbor, who chased us down the road. Luckily for us he was not as "fleet of foot" and we managed to avoid being caught, unfortunately dropping the ill-gotten bottle of milk.

"I know where you're from" the pursuer shouted, "You little urchins, I will report you"! Stealing milk was not the only devious skill acquired through necessity, personally I became proficient at many "devilish acts" during the years spent at "The Princess Alice Home and Orphanage." Periodic hunger and a need to survive often overcame the strict lessons of what was considered right or wrong! Other local trades-people were also going about their business early in the mornings, as we made our way to school. Most of them, early in the war, still delivered goods by horse and cart, such as The Greengrocer with a wagon piled high with all kinds of fresh fruit and vegetables and Window Cleaners carrying buckets, ladders and chamois leathers.

Chimney Sweeps shouldered a stack of long round bristled brushes and the much maligned "Rag and Bone Man" collected anything not wanted, including old clothes, pots, pans, and even long handled wringers or squat obsolete clothes boilers. "Any old rags, pots, pans" he shouted, as his horse slowly meandered down the middle of the road, while a couple of scruffy boys ran after him laughing and shouting, mimicking his call. The most popular by far with us other than the milkman, however, was the baker. His little enclosed wagon with wooden shelves either side was stacked with all kinds of baked goods, including round loaves, long loaves, short, fat loaves, golden brown and glazed, with a delicious just baked aroma. Iced buns, sticky buns, jam tarts, lemon tarts, currant cakes and coconut- covered macaroon pastries, each a different shape and size, literally a scrumptious heaven on wheels and extremely tempting.

The baker stopped his horse frequently at the side of the road, climbing laboriously down from the front seat and moving to the back of the wagon, to drop a little wooden flap and take out a large wicker woven basket. Placing the curved handle over his arm he proceeded to fill it with a variety of items, obviously ordered by residents and after carefully closing the back door set off to make his deliveries.

This was the moment we had been waiting for and the instant he was out of sight, behind a hedge or fence we made our move and dashed toward the cart, while one of us kept watch for his return. Flinging open the little door we hastily jumped up on the back step, reached in and grabbed whatever was close, either a large round loaf or the favorite, a couple of sticky buns or cakes. Hitting the ground again we took off running as fast as we could down the street, until out of sight, we stopped and between gasping breaths consumed our ill-gotten gains. Often, of course, these escapades invariably meant we were late for school with dire consequences, although the punishment received at school was nothing compared to what was doled out for far lesser crimes in the home.

One particularly annoying inconvenience that everyone, including children, suffered during the war, were the horrible little rubber gas masks packed in cardboard boxes, that were suspended by a thin string handle, knotted through holes on each side. Everywhere we went they had to be carried and considering the variety of items the boxes contained, it was probably very fortunate we never actually had to use the masks.

Boys would stuff all kinds of items, too large to fit in their pockets, into the gas mask box, including pieces of stale bread, biscuits, chewing gum and an assortment of "goodies" hidden away for future consumption or disposal. The box became almost like a satchel or a female shoulder bag, with the outside frequently covered with weird drawings and hieroglyphics, the exact meaning of which were known only to the owner or his immediate circle of friends.

Rehearsals were held regularly both at school and back at the home with the awkward abominations, in case of a gas attack, which thankfully never occurred. The practices, however, were inevitably a fun riot and a welcome distraction from lessons, especially when they took place in the school playground with boys and girls together!

The actual masks were made of thick, black, smelly rubber with wide straps tightly stretched over your head. In front a little Plexiglas window fogged up the moment it was pulled on, making them uncomfortable and very difficult to see out. Later models were produced with "Mickey Mouse" ears and softer rubber, owned eventually by younger or some of the "better off" kids at school although we never enjoyed that privilege, but delighted in pulling the ears of those who did! Additionally we made ugly faces and soon discovered that by lifting the front of the mask slightly away from the face, in a sucking motion, the resulting vacuum would expel a very rude "raspberry" causing hysterical giggles from the girls. However, if caught by the sister in charge, a sharp smack across the back of the head instantly ended the joviality.

After the strict discipline of The Orphanage local school rules were a relief and I actually enjoyed the classes while befriending most of the teachers, even my arithmetic teacher who tried hard to make me understand the subject. Like others in the class the occasional piece of chalk was hurled at me for being inattentive or naughty, or even a slap on the back of the hand with a flat ruler, but nothing compared to what was administered so indiscriminately by certain individual House Sisters. School was not coeducational, so even at playtime boys and girls were separated, except for rare meetings to and from The Orphanage, consequently Maurice and I seldom met our sisters, although there were times when the opportunity presented itself immediately after the closing bell, when everyone from "Princess Alice" gathered outside the schoolyard to walk the couple of miles back to the home.

One day each week girls were taught "Home Economics Classes," which often included cooking and baking little items that students were allowed to take home. Both Audrey and Pauline attended these classes at different times and naturally they would inform me and my brother. So on certain days we anxiously waited outside the school gate until they arrived to share with both of us the "Fruits of their Labors". This practice became yet another way of regularly supplementing our normal meager diet, albeit with plain, non-gourmet, but quite wholesome offerings.

At the age of twelve my first "serious" girl friend arrived on one such occasion, after observing the exchange ritual with my sisters she began bringing me samples of her own baking prowess. Even though her cooking was not quite as good as my sisters the habit was encouraged for obvious reasons, and soon our relationship became a little more than just "friendly."

A short while later after sneaking out of the back gate of the orphanage and walking alone a lengthy distance along Chester Road to her house, to be politely informed by her Mother at the front door, that I was a little too young. After having saved hard earned pennies for weeks to take her to the local cinema, the snub was devastating and it took quite a long time to recover from that first rejection, although unless her cooking improved dramatically in later years it was probably just as well the relationship did not continue into the future.

Sutton Park was a huge recreational area situated a short walking distance away from the home and nearly every Sunday, after church, the sister took us for a walk to "get our ozone"! We tramped along footpaths that stretched for miles over gorse, heather and broom-covered hillocks, meandering through woods where bluebells and other seasonal wild flowers grew in abundance. It was great fun just running in the woods, kicking over the fallen leaves and gathering up prickly Horse Chestnuts, which were cracked open to expose the white kernel, which eventually became a prized play-weapon. Occasionally we would find real edible brown-shelled chestnuts, devoured ravenously on the spot and if enough, stashed in our bulging pockets or gas mask boxes for later. Eventually, however, the continuing war changed the whole nature of things, when an open area in the park was taken over by the English Army as a camp for prisoners of war, and a training ground for locally barracked troops with the recently arrived American allies.

Once the area had been commandeered by joint armed forces we often saw columns of British soldiers, passing the home on route marches, always singing popular songs but frequently changing the lyrics. One example was; "It's the wrong way to tickle Mary"! Instead of the original "It's a long way to Tipperary." Naturally, being young impressionable boy's we too soon mimicked the changes, much to the chagrin of the house sisters who accompanied us on walks.

The once beautiful park gradually became more frequently used and abused by military activities during the war, including the erection of anti-aircraft gun emplacements, concrete pillboxes and areas where huge, gray, hippopotamus-shaped Barrage Balloons with floppy fins floated high in the sky, tethered by long wires from metal stakes set deep in the ground. Vast, picturesque natural areas were torn up into grotesque, muddy, undulating stretches by lumbering, camouflaged tanks and armored vehicles with huge white stars painted on the sides, now suddenly using the grounds as a "Military Training Area." Keep out signs were posted at strategic points throughout the park, which of course we frequently ignored whenever let out alone.

Most of the military vehicles were operated by American Servicemen, who by this time late in 1942 had arrived in England, eventually to become part of the great "D Day" invasion force which landed on the Normandy Beaches in June of 1944. The local populace however, particularly "pub-crawlers" and street loungers, verbally acknowledged that booted troops and heavy equipment were systematically destroying the once beautiful natural parklands.

I personally agreed with this sympathy after stepping on a broken coke bottle, suspected to have been carelessly discarded by one of our allies, in the little paddling lake we used to play in. The incident caused an almost-severed big toe, leaving a nasty scar carried to this day, although at the time it was considered almost a war injury by friends.

Local children and we "Orphans" generally liked the Americans, because whenever we met them outside on the street, or they passed in huge canvass topped, camouflaged trucks, they waved and threw sweets or packets of gum to us, creating a frantic scramble on the ground. "Got any gum Yank", we would shout and more often than not they generously responded in kind.

For some obscure reason at the time, nearby resident adults didn't quite share our affection for the soldiers, even though they obviously spent a great deal of money in local shops during the day and pubs, particularly after nightfall.

Later we were informed that the typical "British Reserve" was offended, because it was considered 'bad taste' or even offensive to blatantly "throw money about". It was also obvious that younger, uniformed servicemen attracted local available females, "while our boys were over there fighting"! My brother and I, of course, were not really aware of these opinions at the time and actually benefited very well from visiting servicemen, particularly while venturing out occasionally unaccompanied into The Sutton Park.

Just inside the park gates on the other side of the woods, the large area that had been taken over included rows of khaki colored tents, erected between little, metal roofed outbuildings called Nissan Huts, forming a large compound surrounded by a high barbed wire fence. It was rumored Italian or Austrian prisoners of war were kept there, although we never discovered their exact nationality. On the few occasions we were able to sneak out, usually on Saturday afternoons, we would make our way to the park just to see if anything exciting was happening. It was strictly forbidden to leave The Orphanage grounds but we did it anyway and of course risked the consequences if caught.

Saturday afternoon was an ideal time to try any adventure, because if current behavior had been acceptable we were allowed out in fine weather to play for a few hours, or watch an adjacent football game in progress, until tea time at four o'clock, giving us plenty of time for planned mischief.

The prisoner compound was we understood patrolled by Home Guard, a volunteer organization made up from older ex-servicemen or those considered not fit for active service. The guards were recruited early during the war, to replace regular soldiers posted abroad to the fighting front. Eventually we became very friendly with a couple and the guards never seemed to mind when we talked through the wire fence with the internees, who always appeared reasonably well fed and clean, even in their drab, gray uniforms. Some of them, in broken English, spoke about their own children at home and showed us faded, creased pictures carried in their breast pockets.

Learning we were from the nearby Orphanage they became very sympathetic, obviously thinking we were all orphaned by the war, although we never actually enlightened them.

The American soldiers seemed to come and go as they pleased, and on stolen trips to the park we often saw them walking in a group, or sometimes in the company of a "lady." Very early on we discovered the close proximity of one or two young boys at certain inopportune moments was not always desirable, particularly when the location and the moment for the soldier and his female companion were, in fact, very opportunistic!

"Ghastly Boys" literally stalked any loving couple spotted walking over the soft, moss- covered mounds still surviving among the gorse, until they eventually stopped and sat down presuming they were alone. At that precise moment we appeared from behind a bush to simply stand close and stare innocently, wide-eyed, unblinking with one thought in mind, how much would they offer us to go away?

Eventually, after offers of candy or bribes of gum didn't persuade us to "take a hike" an exasperated, "Hey sonny how about if I give you half-a-crown to go some place else"? The coin was more money than we had ever seen, let alone spend, so hastily grabbing the loot we ran off, laughing, to find another couple. This practice became known as "Fluff Hunting," although I was never quite sure why. For a privileged few during one long summer, however, it was a very profitable pastime and my meager share of the ill-gotten gains was safely hidden away, to be used to very good advantage at a later date.

As the war progressed and air raids became more frequent, concern for the safety of the children increased, in particular the problem of getting everyone out of the house in the event of an emergency. Subsequently each house had a long slide installed made of thick canvas material, stitched over curved metal hoops, extending from a mid-level corridor to the ground below. Everyone lined up at the window opening to sit and slide down to safety, one at a time, similar to the escape exits on modern airplanes. Rehearsals were held regularly and were great fun, especially for boys, seeing the sisters sliding down desperately trying to hold their billowing skirts tightly over spidery black-stocking legs and knee-length bloomers. Fortunately we never experienced an occasion to use the slide in an actual bombing attack that came close enough to warrant it.

At the height of the air raids, a decision was made to evacuate younger children away from the cities to safer, temporary locations in the country. Thousands were evacuated from areas close to major industrial towns and cities, throughout the United Kingdom, by order of the government. Many of those chosen to leave had never seen the countryside before, or farm animals, so it became a whole new experience for them to live in temporary homes as family members, away from larger industrial built up areas.

The Orphanage was located on the outskirts of Birmingham close to Coventry, two Midland cities repeatedly targeted by the Germans, so we were obviously considered in harms way. The decision was therefore eventually made that a few children at a time, from each house, would benefit from a brief stay in the country with a foster family. By some miracle in the late summer of 1941 I was chosen by a kind, smartly-dressed elderly lady, whom I deliberately smiled at appealingly when she visited the home to select suitable candidates. Apparently the local council had designated certain individuals from the Women's Voluntary Service to carry out this special wartime duty. The W.V.S Organization had been formed early on in the war to help relieve hardships suffered as a result of bombing and shortages all over Britain, including distributing clothing and household items. The ladies also organized mobile canteens in city centers and found temporary shelters and homes for bombed out families and evacuees.

Together with a coach-load of other fortunate's we were driven to the county of Derbyshire, where we were separated into pairs and escorted to individual homes in a little farming village alongside the broad banks of the River Trent. It was the first time since coming to the home, I had ever made a long coach journey on such deep luxurious seats, able to snuggle down and sleep practically the whole length of the journey north, up into the beautiful green hills of security. Upon arrival, together with my friend Johnny Butterworth, we were placed in a picturesque little stone cottage owned by the Morton Family, located alongside a winding country lane close to a farming village. It was a country postcard house with a little white picket fence, encompassing a garden full of tall Hollyhocks and masses of multi-colored flowers, surrounding a lush green sloping front lawn.

Clinging to the pebble-dashed walls outside my little attic bedroom, honeysuckle grew in abundance and every evening the heavy sweet scent wafted through the open window. In the narrow country lane, a man wearing Wellington Boots, a tweed jacket and rakish flat cap, guided a small herd of cow's every morning to the nearby pasture, where they grazed contentedly before returning at dusk. Watching fascinated he drove them ahead with a long stick, while across the fields along the tree-lined banks of the River Trent, tall weeping willows dipped and swayed in the morning breezes.

At breakfast-time real honeycomb was placed on the table, collected from their own beehives in the garden by Mister Morton. Wafer thin slices of homemade toasted bread were spread with farm churned butter and succulent honey, followed by a cool freshly churned glass of dairy milk. These were luxury items seldom seen before, other than on the sister's dining table and then only to drool at. The Morton's house was truly a wonderful place and both mother and daughter were forever included among the kindest people known to me, practicing their deep religious beliefs without preaching but by example. If any persons were capable of persuading me to believe in the Methodist religion it would have been the Morton's.

Unfortunately the same couldn't be said for her grandson, who happened to be staying there at the same time. A few years older and obviously better fed, evidenced by his ample girth and very heavy breathing, he was also extremely jealous and antagonistic towards the unwanted "intruders!" He made it very clear from the start that our presence was resented and at every opportunity showed his displeasure in a number of different ways. At the meal table he frequently grabbed greedily for food immediately it was placed down, exhibiting surprisingly bad manners, which immediately brought forth a strong rebuke from either his Grandmother or Aunt. Our more disciplined upbringing, on the other hand, had taught us to wait until invited or at least make a polite request before helping ourselves, even though the daily fare consisted of so many unaccustomed delightful delicacies. Unfortunately our kind hostess often used us as an example of how he should behave, although obviously not gratefully accepted by him.

After meals, when playing out in the back garden, the chubby boy would show his resentment by trying to bully us, using his extra strength of years and sheer overweight to wear us down. The lush back lawn descended in a series of terraces each roughly a foot lower, making it difficult to maintain balance, particularly when barged at by such a weighty individual. On my own extreme difficulty was experienced extricating myself from beneath his flab, whenever he wrestled me to the ground. However, with the aid of my loyal home friend and ally, he was always thwarted by our combined efforts.

During our very brief time spent with the country family we enjoyed many unaccustomed freedoms and kindnesses, which we realized undoubtedly must have been experienced by most other, non-institutionalized, children with caring parents. Unfortunately, all too soon it ended, returning to the rigors of The Orphanage and the continuing sights and sounds of the ongoing war. But at least we retained many unaccustomed happy memories that helped us survive. Personally the wonderful Morton family from Derbyshire was never forgotten, although we were never able to meet again.

Children outside house born in 1933

Maurice and John. Seaside 1934

Yvonne, Joan, John, Pauline, Maurice, Audrey. 1935

John with Grandma 1935

John and Maurice 1937

Sunday walk in the park with Head Sister, 1939

Mothers summer visit 1939

Pauline, John, Maurice, Audrey 1940

Church and Offices Princess Alice Home

The Author 1945

7

Morning Chores

Every weekday morning after breakfast and before morning prayers in church, all boys had to complete a pre-set task in the house. Jobs were allocated on a weekly schedule, regularly changed, including a variety of tasks depending on a boy's age. Some were enjoyable, like clearing dishes from the Sisters' dining table or washing up the cooking utensils because of any "leftovers." A slice of cold toast left in the silver toast rack, with a dab of marmalade added, or even a discarded fatty bacon rind, were infinitely better than our usual fare.

One day at about nine years of age it became my turn to wash up the huge black iron cooking pots, left in the kitchen from the previous day. As usual the deep metal sink was piled high with saucepans to be scraped clean with a thick metal scourer, using thin shavings of yellow soap from a tall earthenware jar and hot water to remove the congealed grease. Invariably the water ran cold before the job was completed, making it very difficult to finish successfully, leaving a thin greasy film over everything. Two boys worked side by side, wearing heavy oilskin aprons to protect their clothing, whilst scraping and scouring the heavy cast iron pans. The one advantage to this particular job, as previously mentioned, was that any left-over tasty morsel one managed to retrieve was hastily consumed. A dried up baked potato, a slither of meat or a crust of pie left at the bottom of a dish, was pounced upon by the one most observant.

On this particular morning, Johnny Butterworth, always considered my best friend, was working with me and at one point I picked up a frying pan to find a crispy piece of bacon stuck in thick fat on the bottom. At precisely the same moment we both reached for it and struggled for possession, until eventually I managed to pull the pan free and grab the desirable mouthful. Stuffing it into my mouth and gobbling it greedily down obviously annoyed him, because a few moments later I realized how upset he was.

Without warning he suddenly placed the flat blade of a broad dinner knife, he had heated over the stove-top gas flame, straight down onto the back of my hand, causing me to yell in pain. The noise attracted the attention of Sister Nellie lurking in the hallway, prompting her to rush in and slap both my ears, adding insult to injury. A while later, after showing her the burnt blistering flesh, a finger-full of margarine was slapped on the wound, further aggravating the pain. After licking it off and dousing it with cold water, somewhat easing the agony, I still carry an obvious triangular scar on the back of my right hand to this day.

Other early jobs before school included sweeping, polishing, or scrubbing floors, depending on the surface. Wooden floors were wiped over with a thick red greasy polish, left to dry and then polished with a large folded cloth, while tiled surfaces were scrubbed with a stiff, bristle brush dipped in a bucket of soapy water. Both tasks involved painfully kneeling on a thin rolled-up cloth pad. The most hated chore definitely was cleaning the downstairs toilet and washbasins. Some early morning jobs were obviously easier, took less time and were not as dirty, making me wonder if the worst ones were kept especially for boys who were repeatedly naughty, because seldom ever was it my privilege to get one of the cushier jobs.

One task always dreaded because it was impossible to avoid getting filthy, even when wearing a protective oilskin apron, was cleaning the dining room stove The large black iron stove in one corner had a dual purpose of heating water in the radiators and keeping the metal tea kettle and various other pots boiling on top. It also supposedly heated the dining room, whenever the little double doors covering the front grill were open. However, unfortunately directly in front of the stove the Sisters' table was positioned, which invariably blocked most of the heat from the remainder of the room.

Every day the stove was cleaned with sticky, black grate polish, poured from a metal can, applied with a stiff-bristled wooden brush until dry, then brushed again with softer bristles until it glistened like coal. If the stove was cold or lukewarm the polish dried slowly, allowing a quick easy polishing, but hot the liquid sent off a foul smelling steam and was very difficult to shine. Either way one's hands or clothes were always smudged and stained with the inky black substance.

Keeping the fire going on cold days was in itself a responsible task and woe-be-tide anyone who allowed it to burn too low. It was one boy's job before school to ensure it was stoked up with coal or coke from a nearby hopper, filled daily. Fuel was delivered by lorry regularly from an outside supplier and deposited in large concrete bunkers situated at the rear of each house.

Men wearing black leather hoods suspended across their foreheads and draped down their backs, carried large hemp sacks and tipped the coal into a small hatch on top of the bunker. Needless to say, the job of filling the fireside hopper and carrying it from the outside bunker was one of the worst winter jobs, particularly in the rain or snow.

In the long narrow "Boot Room" at the rear of the house, a shiny red-tiled floor covered the whole area, extending to stacked rows of wooden box-shelves at one end. Each box displayed a number, signifying where each individual owner's boots had to be placed every day after returning from school, because wearing boots in any other part of the house was not allowed. Two boys every morning cleaned and polished over twenty pairs of dirty lace-up boots, before replacing them back in the correct boxes. Not an easy task, especially when wet boots were invariably covered with caked-on mud, which laboriously had to be scraped off first.

Black boot polish was applied with a worn out, short bristled brush then shone with an old piece of thick toweling. Inevitably dollops of wet mud mixed with the sticky black polish fell onto the floor and eventually stuck, plainly visible on the bright red tiles. Whoever had the job of scrubbing the floor found it very difficult to remove the mess, especially on wet days! Armed only with the antiquated, bristle-less brush and freezing cold water, even the intense pointed application of a long bar of red carbolic soap, which painfully blistered the skin, could not eliminate the black marks. Fortunately one bright boy came up with a solution to the problem, by producing a wide metal spatula, probably stolen, shaped like a putty knife and ideal for scraping underneath the deposits and flicking them off. A final wipe-over with the long-handled wet mop, completed the chore for the duty Sister's final inspection.

Older boys, who had been at the house longer, had invented devious little tricks which were initially performed on and eventually adopted in turn by new boys. Early on these fiendish games would often get younger followers into trouble with the Sisters and sometimes other boys, before learning how to avoid being caught. The most popular prank involved deliberately mixing and replacing different pairs of boots in the cubbyholes after cleaning. It wasn't enough just to place a pair of boots in the wrong box, a genuine enough mistake, but to actually find odd sizes or two left boots in one's box created utter confusion to individual owners. This in particular at a time when everyone was rushing to get ready for school, which, of course, only added to the humorous delight of the instigators who, of course, had no trouble finding their own boots. All footwear issued were the same ankle-length, black lace-up boots, which frequently had been handed down from an older boy and nearly always were either too large, too loose causing blisters, or too small cramping your toes. The inevitable problems derived from squeezing feet into ill-fitting boots and having to walk long distances to school and back caused me to suffer for years. Whenever possible they were removed unabashedly beneath the desk to relieve the agony, only to panic when the recess bell rang while struggling to get them back on, prompting laughter from more fortunately attired affluent local classmates.

On one particular April first, having just turned eleven, the act of peeling potatoes from a metal bucket was my designated task. The bucket contained the average daily requirement for the house, amounting to over a dozen pounds of spuds to be peeled with a very blunt wooden handled peeler. As each potato was finished they were deposited into a separate bucket of cold water and taken to the kitchen when full. The Sister on duty always inspected the contents to ensure each potato had been peeled properly, with no black eyes or dark spots and the bucket was indeed brim-full before it was removed. On this particular "April Fool's Day," a friend had dared me to play a traditional trick on the Duty Sister, who at the time happened to be Sister Nellie Hunter, who had recently replaced Sister Eileen Holloway. The new Head Sister's assistant, Sister Eva, was always more lenient and forgiving and certainly more likely to take a joke. Whereas Sister Nellie, the short, plump, red-faced, middle-aged lady with the northern accent, whom we soon discovered possessed a wonderful singing voice, unfortunately also had a very quick temper which frequently flared up at the slightest prompting.

Unlike Sister Eva, the newcomer seldom ever found time to talk to any of us except to scold, or punish, for even the slightest misdemeanor or excuse. All Sisters wore dark blue uniforms with stiff white starched collars, cuffs and a broad, stiff cloth sash around the waist. Sister Nellie, however, wore a thick, but narrower leather belt with a large metal ring sewn in, from which hung a bunch of long, heavy, iron door keys.

The jangling of these keys often warned us of her approach, especially at night when she often attempted to creep up the stairs to catch us talking, or out of bed. Thankfully the posted lookout at the door had been previously warned, that the sixth step from the bottom creaked badly, particularly when it fully bore her excessive weight.

Boys being boys a dare is a dare, and once dared you were honor-bound to carry it out or be branded a coward! So one early morning the idea was conceived to simply play an "April Fool's" joke, by pretending to have peeled potatoes, but instead merely transferring them unpeeled into another bucket. At the appropriate moment, glancing around to ensure Sister Eva was still close by in the hallway, knowing full well the joke would be better received by her I loudly called out "Sister I've finished!"

Before the words were hardly out of my mouth, to my horror, Sister Nellie stepped out from the doorway where she had been standing half-hidden. "I will check, Sister!" she exclaimed, signaling to her assistant as she bustled across the hallway to peer over my kneeling form into the tall container. Summoning up all my courage, turning and looking up into the expressionless tight-lipped face staring down at me I gasped, "April Fool," half whispering almost apologetically, trying to smile.

There was an infinite moment of complete silence as scrubbing and polishing brushes stopped and heads turned to stare, waiting. This was the dare! The ultimate! The test! Bending closer for a better view of the contents of the bucket, Sister Nellie's face puffed and flushed an even-brighter red than normal as her eyes narrowed.

"I suppose you think that's funny?" she hissed. "Well, I don't!"

Whereupon she kicked out with a black-stocking-covered leg, sending the bucket flying and the un-peeled wet potatoes rolling higgledy-piggledy across the tiled floor, at the same instant striking me with the large ring of iron keys deftly unclipped from her belt. At the second swipe I instinctively ducked, but too late as the keys dug painfully into my scalp, causing me to flinch at the pain while desperately attempting to stem swelling tears.

"Now pick them up and peel!" she angrily exclaimed. "Don't try and April fool me?"

Painfully crawling around on my knees to pick them up one at a time and drop them back into the bucket, I slowly started peeling again. The pain was acute, cautiously putting one hand up to my head, as the blood began to ooze through my fingers, plopping into the reddening water. Eventually, somehow the task was completed and this time reported to Sister Eva, who thankfully was still nearby. After checking the contents she took me into the bathroom opposite to bathe my head with a cold flannel, temporarily stemming the bleeding, before an iodine-dipped swab was applied to the wound which stung sharply. Later, walking on the way to school, my companions who either saw or heard of my "dare," swamped me with praise and slapped me on the back. Unfortunately the scars on the back of my head remain to the present, as a reminder of that particular "April Fool's Day."

Another incident involving Sister Nellie took place in the bathroom some time later during the war, on one cold winter morning before breakfast. As a young pre-teen the habit of using "bad words" or expletives had yet to be developed, in fact it was seldom any boy at the home uttered profanities such as one finds commonly expressed by certain teens today. Not until years later, after joining up as a fourteen-year-old "Boy Soldier," did the meaning of particular "four letter words," along with many other crude "barrack room" expressions and practices, become familiar to me. There were however, certain expressions or idioms peculiar to the Midlands, often used to describe our feelings or dislike for particular individuals or incidents, especially words and sayings picked up from older "role models." Words like damn or sod, to express annoyance, bloody, such as in "bloody fool!" or "bugger," a vulgarism often used without even knowing the real meaning. All used under certain circumstances, almost involuntarily, as expressions of frustration at one's own incompetence.

To Sister Nellie, however, the use of these words was considered extreme profanity, punishable by a particularly drastic method, devised and carried out instantly by her, after overhearing such "nasty devilish language." At a much younger age, having previously observed older boys suffering her extreme personal punishment, I had cringed watching, sickened at the sight, never believing it would ever happen to me but unfortunately it did.

The task of cleaning the white enameled washbasins and bathtub was a revolting chore, second only to the lavatories. Greasy gray scum marks were always left on the sides and rim, together with dried, spat-on pink dentifrice powder, extremely difficult to remove particularly with just cold water, which unfortunately was all that could be drawn from the tap after twenty boys had concluded morning ablutions. Foot-long bars of red carbolic soap were used which contained a caustic, phenol, crystalline benzene compound, used today in making plastics and insecticides. The soap supposedly removed grease and was applied with a hard bristle scrubber to all such surfaces, including the red floor tiles throughout the house. Unfortunately, after only a few moments of use the skin on bare hands invariably turned red, blistered and very sore.

On one particularly cold winter morning, having almost finished cleaning the final basin, my hand scraped across the rough edge of a metal tap, lacerating the skin, causing the blood to flow freely from the wound and swirl with the water down the drain. Involuntarily I let out a cry followed by a brief curse. Memory is vague as to the exact expletive but unfortunately Sister Nellie, who as usual was lurking unnoticed in the background, overheard it.

"What did you say boy?" She demanded upon entering the room.

"I cut my hand Sister!" I pathetically replied vaguely holding it aloft.

"I asked what you said not what you did!"

"Ouch?" I volunteered sheepishly.

"You swore! What happens to boys who swear?"

Knowing what happened I wasn't about to remind her.

"I will not have boys blaspheming!" she exclaimed angrily, bustling threateningly toward me. "You have a filthy mouth and we must cleanse it!" Grabbing the back of my neck with a pudgy hand and the bar of caustic soap with the other, she attempted to cram the square end into my mouth. Tightening my lips and clenching my teeth, with some difficulty I managed to prevent the vile tasting object from actually entering, while struggling desperately, trying to escape her grasp, but to little avail.

Obviously Sister was grossly larger than my-less-than four-foot frame, and the sheer weight of her bulky, voluminous body, together with adult strength forced my head downwards. The acid taste from the carbolic soap inside my mouth was revolting, and beginning to vomit violently over the side of the washbasin caused my hurried release.

"Next time watch your language! Now clean that filthy mess up!" She commanded.

As the sister left the room handfuls of cold water were gulped into my mouth, attempting to flush away the poisonous mixture. Certainly those two encounters with Sister Nellie did nothing to improve my respect for her, but worse was to follow!

One task the Sisters performed regularly, which most certainly they disliked as much as we did, was "Bug-Raking" a name given to the process of washing and shaving heads for nits, lice and fleas. With so many boys in the house and hygiene not always so vigorously enforced as it should have been, nature happened and a monthly ritual was introduced. Inspection took place in the bathroom, where we were lined up with bowed heads, praying of course nothing would be found. If any "creepy-crawlies" were discovered heads were shaved with hand-operated clippers and blunt scissors, which in the Sisters inexperienced hands tore and dug rather than clipped. Naked heads were soaked and soaped with a foul-smelling shampoo, then dusted with a dry powder that stung the scalp for days afterwards. Boys who underwent the balding process were obvious victims of much ridicule, particularly at the nearby secondary modern school, where any excuse for hurling an insult at us "orphans" was always welcomed by the locals.

The most hated job of all at any time was cleaning the squat porcelain toilet at the end of the cloakroom, a task designated usually for a recently committed misdemeanor. The single downstairs toilet was used quite frequently during the day, but in particular at night, when the lone chamber pot in the bedroom was full or a boy wanted to do "number twos." With so much traffic in the course of twenty-four hours, from an equivalent number of boys, the chain-pull flush was hardly ever silent. Younger boys in particular were not always so careful in their jet stream aim, or where they actually deposited the stiff brown, recycled sheets of toilet paper, either before or after use! Frequently the toilet was blocked, with the inevitable overflow of the contents across the tiled floor, often spreading under the half door, across the tiled floor into the cloakroom to lap against the bottom wooden drawers. A large mop and bucket were used to soak the mess up and wipe the floor with a strong smelling, tar-based disinfectant added to the water. The obnoxious odor frequently permeated the whole house but that particular room always stunk! Often the wooden seat and bowl were spattered with feces, which had to be cleaned with a stiff - bristled, long-handled brush, then wiped with a rag soaked in the disinfectant; definitely not a job one vied for! However, over the years I became quite proficient at the job, having more than my fair share of practice, proving very useful later in life, during my teenage basic military training along with thirty two other young recruits.

Not all jobs were allocated on weekdays, as some took more time and had to be completed on Saturdays after breakfast, before being allowed out to play. Depending on whether or not one was in trouble during the current week would determine the type of task, also the nature of the crime dictated the severity and length of punishment, which could last all morning and involve more than one boy. The loss of Saturday morning play privileges outside meant a great deal, as it was one of a very few chances to meet with friends from other houses, and in my case a rare opportunity to see my brother or sisters. Invariably, one or other of us siblings would have been restricted indoors for some minor misdemeanor that had offended our keepers.

Very early on it became evident that my sister Audrey, for some unknown reason, always seemed to avoid serious confrontations and punishment, perhaps being the elder among the four of us and of a less tempered nature, she had probably learned the art of restraining her emotions when provoked.

Later it became even more difficult for us to meet because of "junior apprentice" commitments in one of the support utilities on The Orphanage grounds. The Bakery, Laundry, Hospital and Farm all "employed" teenager's, similar to the Vegetable Gardens and even the Church and Infant School. Each of us worked in one or another of these locations at some time during our years at the home. Supposedly these jobs were designed to teach future trades to those so engaged, but they also denied us so many necessary childhood freedoms and outdoor playtime with friends and siblings.

Children fortunate enough not to be so preoccupied with chores would play games like netball for the girls (similar to basketball) or soccer for boys, which in the summer months would be replaced by swimming lessons or cricket. If not athletically inclined one met with friends, or perhaps inevitably became involved in some form of childish mischief, often resulting in trouble and even more isolation or punishment.

The individual desire to leave The Orphanage compound and venture into the big wide world outside was frequently overpowering, often leading me back into trouble if caught. However, gradually developing in age and cunning, I became much more adept at avoiding discovery.

8

The Chestnut Tree

Towards the end of the twentieth century a very popular song called YMCA, used hand and arm movements to shape letters simultaneously as they were sung. In the 1940s there was another popular wartime music hall melody titled, "Under the Spreading Chestnut Tree," when singers also used similar gestures to describe "Chest, Nut and Tree," by placing their hands on their chests, heads and extending them in the air to imitate branches. Whenever a group of people congregated in a party mood the song was invariably performed with great gusto. It was also actively promoted, although probably not written, by Lord Baden Powel the founder of the Boy Scout movement in England. Most certainly we always sang it at all campfire sing-a-longs attended as a young Cub Scout.

Except for the title this has nothing to do with the following story, but it reminded me of an incident involving the massive, inspiring Chestnut Tree that stood in all its grandeur in the center of the infant school play area. In spring it was festooned with thousands of cone shaped, white blooms, eventually becoming prickly seed horse chestnuts, which gave generations of young boys so much pleasure but almost caused my younger brother's early demise.

One Saturday morning, shortly after Maurice had joined me in Meriden House, an incident occurred in the upper playground that almost parted us forever and actually placed a second member of the family in hospital for a considerable length of time.

After completing my scheduled early morning chore and looking forward to going out to play with friends, a boy from another house came running up to the back door breathlessly calling out to me. "Your kid's fallen out the Conker Tree, they've called the hospital"! (The local nickname all brothers called each other was "Our Kid")

Being very familiar with the location I immediately rushed to the top playground where the giant Horse Chestnut Tree stood centered, encircled by tall, pointed top, iron railings. Beneath the imposing leafy splendor of the tree, a group of boys stood surrounding a crumpled figure lying prone on the hard tarmac.

Elbowing my way through I stumbled past a uniformed sister bending over the sprawled body of my brother, lying horribly twisted on one side. A couple arrived with a wooden twin-handled canvas stretcher, and the sister ordered four of the senior boys to carry him across the large green oval to the hospital. Unfortunately in the process of lifting him by his shoulders and legs, the bigger boys who obviously were not trained medically, or had ever been instructed in the practice, were not too careful. Urgency was uppermost in their minds, so consequently what may have at first been simple fractures, actually resulted in the ends of broken bones penetrating the outer skin! Luckily Maurice knew little of this after having passed out. Proving fortunate at the time, considering how he was lifted and the ultimate method of transportation designated a short while later.

The Assistant Governor, Mr. Roycroft, arrived afterwards and decided, due to the multiple fractures, the patient should be transported to the larger Public Children's Hospital, located a few miles distant, in the nearby city of Birmingham. With his leg in a temporary splint and now fully awake, Maurice was laid on the back seat of the Governor's little black saloon car to be driven downtown, proving an experience he was never going to forget. Unfortunately the hospital on home grounds did not possess an ambulance and this being wartime, most of the local medical transport was invariably kept busy elsewhere in the district.

The one and only reason Maurice had climbed the tree that particular morning was to augment his personal stock of Horse Chestnuts, from which a large single seed was carefully extracted and ripened for the game known as "Conkers", (believed to be derived from the local slang word conk, meaning to strike.)

After harvesting suitably ripe specimens, the prickly outer skin was carefully broken open and the large white seed removed, which once exposed to the air quickly turned a dark, shiny brown. A nail was driven through the center making a hole, through which a string was threaded, then double-knotted at one end, to prevent it coming off when violently swung. An opponent would dangle his own weapon at arms-length by the end of the string, while an attempt was made to strike and hopefully shatter it, by carefully taking aim and swinging down hard with ones own projectile. The game became quite sophisticated in time, when it was discovered how the outer skin could be hardened, either by baking in the sun, on the stove, or more scientifically soaking in malt vinegar, whenever the rare condiment could be somehow procured.

This process invariable decided the winner and also the status an individual "Conker" earned. For example if ten of the opponent's weapons were shattered, one's own became a "Tenner" or "Twentier" etc. These dried, wrinkled and dented seeds were very prized sought-after personal belongings, frequently vigorously bartered for in swapping sessions and one of a very few affordable playthings.

However, some weeks later, after returning to The Orphanage hospital, Maurice described to me exactly what had happened whilst stretching along the high, narrow branch and grabbing for that particular large Horse Chestnut, hanging so temptingly almost beyond his grasp. Apparently, just after he had begun to ascend the tree, a boy was sent by Sister Eva telling him to return to the house and finish scrubbing the bathroom floor, which he had apparently abandoned mid-way through! Maurice responded by shouting to him; "I'll be down in a minute"! Obviously he went down a lot quicker than anticipated!

At the time of the accident a mutual friend, Dave Pollard, had been posted below the tree as a fielder for a game of cricket in progress across the far side of the playground, against the school wall. Unfortunately for him, but fortunately for Maurice, he nearly caught more than was expected. For, as my brother reached forward, the branch he was standing on snapped and he plummeted downwards, striking the stationary boy a glancing blow before hitting the solid tarmac. Except for a badly bruised shoulder the unfortunate catcher was unharmed but "Our Kid" had shattered his leg in three places, causing him to pass out, luckily narrowly missing the sharp points at the top of the iron railings, where he could have been firmly impaled.

When the Assistant Governor finally began the journey to the Birmingham Children's Hospital it was dark, and blackout rules demanded that all headlights should be shaded, making it a little dangerous to drive. As a result, whenever the driver braked or swerved, as was the case quite frequently to avoid other vehicles, Maurice was catapulted off the rear seat and painfully deposited on the car floor, each time managing somehow to struggle back. Thousands of fatal accidents, involving badly lit vehicles in cities and country roads, occurred during the frequent air-raid blackouts.

After finally arriving at the hospital, which he described as a huge cathedral-like forbidding building, his leg was put in traction and plastered from hip to ankle.

Doctors had a great deal of trouble applying splints and apparently did not consider the leg would ever mend correctly. After a surprisingly brief stay, however, he was returned by more comfortable transport back to the "Princess Alice" cottage hospital, where the leg and his ego eventually healed. Unfortunately, the length of time spent away from school meant he missed the upcoming "Eleven-Plus" school exam, where passing would have entitled him to acceptance into the highly regarded local Grammar School, with a number of his closest friends.

Nearly every boy looked forward to being accepted into this particular school, not only because of the education but also the privilege of wearing smart blazer uniforms, with color ringed peaked caps. The luxury of clean long socks every day and short serge trousers without the usual ugly patch in the seat was also a major plus! In addition grammar school lunches were infinitely more edible and nourishing than those normally dished up back in the home. For what it was worth I never managed to attend that elite institution either, or enjoy the benefits afforded a bright eleven-year-old, albeit for slightly different reasons. My education continued to advance rapidly however, in a direction and in subjects designed more for survival and escape, rather than academia.

Whilst Maurice was still convalescing, my sisters and I visited at weekends and were permitted to push him in his wheelchair around the path encircling the oval, on the head nurses insistence that he needed to have "fresh air". He sat in the canvas wheelchair bolt upright with his plaster-encased leg lying on an extended seat board, sticking straight out in front like a battering ram. During one visit pushing him at quite a high rate of speed, wearing a pair of metal well- oiled roller skates, head down barreling forward along the concrete path, I failed to see the Assistant Governor standing in front of the church until almost too late. Very narrowly avoiding impaling the staff member's broad stern by inches, brushing close by and causing him to spin around almost losing his balance. Needless-to-say he was not a happy man!

It was explained quite firmly, with every word accompanied by a flat handed slap to the back of my head that the risk taking could have caused more serious injury, both to my brother or anyone else struck by the outstretched solidly encased limb.

Following the incident Maurice was never perambulated again wearing roller skates, but only at a leisurely flat-footed walk for the remainder of his confinement. That particular lesson was well learnt but it was not to be the last time the Governors anger would be enflamed!

After a lengthy period of recuperation Maurice and I were finally reunited back in Meriden, under the watchful eye of Sister Nellie, whom we were both shortly to unintentionally antagonize yet again. The following, perfectly innocent pastime, created an incident that finally separated us, not only during the remainder of our stay at the home, when we were able to still meet occasionally on the grounds, but eventually permanently until decades afterwards.

There were two upper landings in Meriden House, one on the top floor where the attic storage cupboards and Pressing Room were and the other on the second floor which extended from the senior boy's bedroom at the rear, to the sisters room at the front. Both landings came to an abrupt end at the top of two separate, descending flights of stairs leading progressively to the ground floor.

The hard wooden planked floors were covered in thick, shiny linoleum originally a light brown in color, but over the years had become faded and stained by frequent polishing and dirty bare feet! There were also areas where the glossy surface had split and separated from the stiff, raffia-like stitching underneath, causing sharp protrusions to extend upwards. The points often caught exposed toes or dug into the bottom of naked feet, making night creeping a little hazardous, particularly if one were out of bed for any other reason, rather than the obvious. The difficult task of polishing the surface with thick, red wax, accomplished on hands and knees, was a painful experience, but in spite of the hazards a game was invented which made this particular Saturday morning task infinitely more enjoyable, once the required lengthy chore had been completed.

On the top landing between the Pressing Room and storage cupboards, at the end of the hallway, spare blankets and uncased, striped pillows were stored on shelves. The folded red blankets with horse hair pillows placed on top, made excellent cushioned pads for sliding along the landing. By running a few feet and diving flat on one's stomach you were able to slide the full length of the landing, while endeavoring to make the tight turn and bounce down the first flight of stairs to the next level.

The intention was to see who could travel the farthest, although it was seldom either boy actually made the turn. Invariably stopping short and gradually descending, accelerating jarringly to bounce downwards.

The whole process was repeated on the bottom landing without attempting the turn to the ground floor, mainly because of the hard, non-slip tiles at the bottom and also, more importantly, because of the risk of encountering one of the Sisters. Inevitably, if that were to happen it would surely happen to me, which unfortunately it eventually did!

One early autumn Saturday morning Maurice and I had completed the linoleum polishing in record time after breakfast, so before informing the sister on duty, we took the opportunity to pull out the stored blankets and pillows to enjoy one of our favorite past-times. Separately we ran and dived, skidding along the upper floor, turning and sliding down the stairs bouncing to the first landing. Then it was my turn to work up enough speed to reach the top of the stairs leading to the lower hallway, in one run.

Throwing the large pad ahead along the slippery surface and running full tilt, I slid headfirst down the length of the landing, coming to an abrupt stop at the very edge of the last staircase, to peer downwards over the top step at a pair of shiny, black, lace-up shoes. Looking slowly up from the black stocking ankles, above the broad hips and ample bosom, I stared into the stern face rising over the double chin, below the half-closed eyes of Sister Nellie Hunter. Not a pleasant sight!

"What do you think you are doing"? She demanded through tightly-drawn lips.

"Polishing the floor Sister"! I hesitatingly replied.

"We've finished"! I added weakly, starting to rise.

"You may have finished"! She gritted. "But I haven't"! Where-upon she began to flail violently with both arms, beating me around the head with flat, open hands, as I attempted to stand up.

"You are meant to polish not play slide, you horrible little boy"! She screamed between each strike.

"You two are nothing but trouble"! She declared, glancing up at my brother, looking down nervously between the banister rails on the landing above.

My head swung from side to side as multiple double-handed blows rained down, stinging both ears. Somehow managing to stagger to my full height brought me almost level to her stature, given the added advantage of the top step. Instinctively lashing out, flaying defensively with both arms, pushing into the soft folds of her expansive stomach with all the strength possible to muster.

"Stop hitting me"! I shouted defiantly.

Suddenly the myriad of blows dramatically ceased, as pudgy hands shot up into the air and she teetered, tottering on the edge, desperately trying to maintain balance. Inevitably, after what seemed a moment of eternity, her footing gave way as she collapsed sideways, rolling like a giant Barrage Balloon, slowly falling backwards, sliding down the stairs desperately grasping for the handrail with frantic fingers as she fell. Abruptly the fall ended at the bottom on the hard stone floor, her black spidery legs askew with skirts floating aloft, exposing knee length, white laced, voluminous pantaloons. At any other time the scene may have been funny but at that precise moment I was terrified, thinking what may have just happened.

For seeming infinity there was complete silence, while literally holding my breath. Then came a feeble deep-throated groan, followed by a slight quivering movement as Sister slowly stirred, rolling over onto her broad side.

"Sister Eva"! She wailed feebly.

"Sister Eva"! She gasped louder.

"SISTER EVA"! Now screaming, as she struggled precariously to her feet.

At that moment Sister Eva suddenly appeared, running breathlessly out from the adjacent Dining Hall.

"Oh my God what happened"? "Are you alright"? She enquired.

"Send for Mister Brassington"! Nellie Hunter commanded, straightening her skirts, while supporting her bulky frame groggily with both arms against the solid banister post.

"He will deal with you"! She breathlessly declared, pointing an accusing podgy finger up the stairs towards me.

"Go to your bed and stay there until you're sent for"!

Knowing and fearing exactly what was to come I turned back to the landing and morosely entered the bedroom to sit and await my anticipated fate.

On the way glancing up hopelessly at Maurice, still nervously peering between the upper banister railings, fortunately forgotten in the rumpus at least for the time being.

Mister Brassington first arrived at the Orphanage earlier in the war when I was almost ten, it was rumored he was a retired Navel Petty Officer, although this was never actually confirmed. He took up residence with his petite wife in one of a row of tall terraced houses, situated on Chester Road across the road from The Orphanage grounds.

In a similar house in the same row senior girls lived a more privileged existence and attended the local Grammar School. Most of them also sang in the church choir, possibly about the only time us other "poor unfortunates" ever saw them. The one exception was my earlier friendship with the kindly, caring Ruth, who earlier had suffered the unfortunate accident on her bicycle.

Mister Brassington's front door faced the entrance across from the playing fields, frequently used as a quick way out to the local shops, which made it extremely difficult to sneak out unnoticed at certain times. His office window was also located close by in Brampton Hall, adjoining the school, where assembly, concerts and plays were performed on special occasions such as Christmas and Easter.

The hall was normally associated with happier events, but a command visit to his office invariably meant anything but a joyful experience, in fact most boys dreaded it, except maybe the more senior. As a member of staff he was responsible for certain administrative duties, but became primarily known as "The Discipline Master" by the majority of younger boys, who feared and avoided him whenever possible. His wife on the other hand, who had a similar position overseeing the girls, was reportedly a little more lenient and sympathetic towards her young charges. Certainly rumors never circulated about any ill-treatment, or abusive punishment administered by her, from either my sisters or any other girls I became acquainted with.

Thick set and stockier in stature than the taller Governor, he was clean-shaven but with a dark shadowy jutting chin and thick bushy eyebrows, which always made him look fierce. Everyday attire was a dark formal suit, with a stiff white shirt collar and knotted tie that protruded above a buttoned, matching waistcoat. Trousers were always meticulously creased down the front, with turn-ups just touching the highly polished black shoes, completing his normally meticulous outfit.

Habits formed from many years in naval service were obviously ingrained and I cannot recall any instance of him changing his stern, grumpy expression for a semblance of a smile, except in the company of a House Sister or an important visitor. He spoke with a deep northern accent, similar to Sister Nellie Hunter, snapping words out as strict commands rather than requests. Undoubtedly also left over from his years spent at sea, directing lower-ranked members of a ships crew. A talent probably better suited to controlling the inmates of a military institution, rather than young orphaned children!

After having been sent up stairs, nervously sitting on the edge of my bed seemingly for hours, I anticipated his arrival. Lunchtime passed without receiving any food, until finally, upon hearing the sound of someone approaching along the landing, I stood as Sister Eva entered the room. "You are to come down, put on your boots and go over to Brampton Hall"! She informed me softly.

Detecting a hint of sympathy as she spoke, I took the proffered hand as she escorted me down to the lower hallway, out the back door to the outside pathway.

"You must go straight over to the office Mister Brassington is waiting for you"!

"That's what worries me" came the thought.

It wasn't far to the office across the upper playground, past the familiar giant chestnut tree and brick toilets, then through the heavy double doorway into Brampton Hall. Even though sunny outside my body shivered with chilled trepidation, possibly also because of only wearing short, threadbare, serge trousers and a thin woolen pullover.

Cautiously making my way up the steps at the side of the stage, and crossing to the office door displaying his nameplate in the center,

I hesitantly knocked nervously on the thick wooden panel. Hearing no reply, tapping louder a second time and desperately hoping he was not there, a muffled voice seemed to declare what sounded like, "Do come in"!

Turning the shiny, large brass handle and slowly pushing the heavy door open, cautiously I peered inside.

"I said don't come in"! A voice snapped angrily.

The Master was apparently not alone. There was a senior girl recognized as one of the older high school students vaguely known, sitting on the edge of the deep brown leather armchair to one side of his desk.

Appearing very flustered, a hurried attempt was made to tuck the bottom hem of her white blouse into her skirt waist with one hand, while holding the unbuttoned edges together with the other, without much success exposing a white lacy brassiere.

Standing slightly to one side, grappling frantically with his trouser and waistcoat buttons simultaneously with both hands, the Master was also having quite a difficult time due to the pointed end of his shirt protruding from the trouser flap, getting in the way.

Looking unusually ruffled with greasy, black hair hanging limply over his perspiring forehead and necktie askew, he demanded.

"Who are you"? Hastily he stepped behind the desk still struggling frantically with the trouser buttons.

"Davies Sir" I replied, "I was told to come and see you by Sister Nellie"!

"I said in an hour"! He blurted angrily, glancing down at his bulging waistline and flapping shirt.

"Get out and wait"!

Retreating outside and standing in one corner of the stage, I wondered vaguely what kind of punishment was administered to girls causing them both to undress. After a few moments the older girl came out and without even a glance in my direction breathlessly hurried across the stage, down the steps out of sight through the main doorway.

At that moment the office door opened again.

"You can come in now" There came the gruff command.

Nervously entering, standing facing him as he sat down behind the large desk, his appearance now seemed a little more composed.

"So" he exclaimed, drawing the word out. "You are the boy who thinks he can push Sister downstairs"? Angrily he glared at me from beneath thick, bushy eyebrows.

"She was hitting me"! I stammered falteringly.

"Was she really? Well that's just what I am going to do! No excuse for pushing people down stairs! Come here"!

With that he stood and reached for a long, thin bamboo cane from a tall, leather covered umbrella stand by the door, swishing it viciously in the air. "This is going to hurt me more than you!" He explained.

Somehow, at that moment, I doubted the truth of that statement?

"Bend over!" he commanded, pointing to the deep seated leather armchair where the girl had earlier sat. "Take down your trousers"!

From past situations knowing this was reserved for a very serious crime, meekly obeying I slowly bent over the front of the chair. As the first stripe landed my fingers dug into the soft leather and tears welled beneath my eyelids. Five more blows across buttocks and upper thighs caused me to cringe with pain, gritting my jaw refusing to cry out as each stroke was accompanied by a hissed exclamation, "Do-not- push-sister-down-stairs!"

Punishment finally over and gingerly pulling my trousers back over my inflamed posterior I turned defiantly to face him. His expression now even more flushed and breathing labored, after this additional latest physical exertion.

"Now go back to your house and don't ever let me see you here again boy, do you understand?" He puffed.

Exiting gratefully, slowly stumbling from backside agony towards the house and Nellie Hunter, who immediately commanded me upstairs to the bedroom for the remainder of the day. Actually it brought relief to lie naked beneath the cold cotton sheets on my stomach, easing the burning welts which lasted for days afterwards. The staircase episode later became notorious, with the tale repeated quite often following numerous questions and many suggestions, making me somewhat of a hero among other boys.

In time I became very accustomed to the "go to bed" routine and over the years many unique ways of making the lonesome experience more enjoyable were developed. A whole new fantasy world opened up in isolation, further enlarged by a boyhood imagination that helped me survive many, long boring days. Unfortunately so much time spent alone in the future, inevitably involved me in further trouble. Following this particular incident, upon the insistence of Sister Nellie, my brother was permanently moved next door to Seymour House. Once again we were destined to be separated!

9

High Days and Holy Days

Christmas was without doubt an exception to the rule, because it was always the singular most pleasurable time during any year at the home. Whether the Sisters were more lenient or we actually tried harder to behave and stay out of trouble I cannot recall, but there is no recollection of ever being punished over Christmas. Maybe the week before or after but never over the actual holiday, if only we had been treated the same way year round, life may have been more bearable! The Staff all seemed to have a change of heart at this time, becoming more thoughtful, more concerned about our welfare and certainly increasingly pious. A great deal of time was spent relating the Christmas story, particularly to the younger boys, thereby increasing each individual's expectations of what was to come.

Festivities began early on Christmas Eve with a carol service at the church, followed by the whole choir parading around The Oval, stopping at each house in turn under hand-held lanterns to sing carols, as we gathered to watch out of the playroom window. After the singers retired we were given a cup of freshly made hot, milky cocoa and a sweet chocolate whole-meal biscuit, a rare treat usually reserved only for the Sisters. On this night in particular it didn't seem to matter how much noise was made in the bedroom, although eventually the anticipated excitement of the next day lulled us all to sleep earlier than usual.

Unknown to new arrivals at first, the Sisters were kept very busy during the evening stuffing "Santa's" stockings and socks with all manner of goodies. After wrapping and labeling, the multi-shaped gifts were deposited in a large square wicker basket, normally used for laundry or bed linens. Growing older and wiser, we often attempted to stay awake and catch the Sisters creeping upstairs to place a filled stocking on each individual bed. Somehow, however, they always knew exactly when we were all asleep.

Every Christmas morning we awoke to find over-filled stockings at the foot of the bed stuffed with a variety of sweets, fruit and small toys, keeping us all noisily amused until Sister Eva arrived to supervise, as we washed and dressed in our best "Sunday Clothes."

It was a long-held tradition early on this particular morning to gather outside the Head Sister's bedroom, to sing her favorite carols, until she deigned to appear in the doorway. This was also one of the rare occasions Sister Nellie was ever seen to smile, somewhat benevolently upon the assembled throng, while handing out a variety of sweets from an ornamental glass bowl to the young carolers. Following the joyful rendition we were led downstairs to the festively decorated dining hall, now hung with paper chains and numerous large red or gold bells, for a special Christmas breakfast.

The customary hunk of dry bread was fried a deep crusty brown on both sides in beef dripping, then covered with a tablespoonful of scrambled egg made from boxed, dried egg powder. Powdered eggs and milk were commonly used during the war as a substitute for the real thing, even though the farmer daily milked a herd of dairy cows and kept a battery of free range chickens, causing me to often wonder what happened to all those fresh eggs. None-the-less, on this particular morning all plates were bread-wiped clean, although second helpings were never proffered and even the drudgery of morning chores, usually undertaken before breakfast, were excused.

After the unaccustomed wholesome meal, hurrying down the hallway with great excitement into the playroom at the front of the house, we stood surrounding the deep square laundry basket, positioned carefully in the center of the room. The container, overflowing with a variety of multi-shaped, colorfully wrapped packages, was watched over by Sister Nellie. The omnipresent Mr. Salt, whom we never failed to recognize, dressed as "Santa Claus," lifted the gifts out individually and handed one to each excited named recipient. A few fortunate children received gifts sent earlier by relatives, hidden away by the Sisters until this moment. Every boy however, including those without known relatives also received a gift from the home, donated apparently during the year by local concerned residents or benefactors. Brightly-colored wrappings and ribbons were torn off frantically and flung into the empty basket. For a couple of hours bedlam reigned on the playroom floor, as presents were shown, shared and played with, until finally put away in individually numbered square cubbyholes lining one wall.

Throughout the following year gifts would be admired, swapped, damaged, lost or "borrowed," always giving endless moments of simple pleasure to the owners at every snatched opportunity. Designated playtime, however, whether indoors or outside, was usually one of the first privileges to be denied for bad behavior, or if any of the strict rules were ever infringed.

The Christmas Morning Church Service was special in a number of ways. At eleven o'clock, seated in the pews, everyone looked extra clean and naturally on their best behavior after such an unaccustomed hearty breakfast and new exciting gifts. On this occasion the front of the chancel was always decorated with pinecones, holly wreaths and tinsel, while large red bows at the end of each pew added a further festive touch.

The Senior Right Reverend Minister from the Methodist Central Office, whose exact name escapes my memory, but who only graced the home with his austere presence on rare occasions, came attired in full splendid regalia. A long purple stole bearing a large gold cross was draped across his shoulders, adding more color than the usual drab black and white worn by the regular ministers. Even the customary monotonous boring sermon was replaced by the Christmas story, which in spite of hearing many times before we always pretended to listen intently, thereby avoiding the customary swipe about the head for dozing off, or exchanging sidelong raised eyebrow glances with friends. The carols were always fun because most were known from memory and therefore sung rather raucously, particularly when the last verse had a choir descant, which we always felt compelled to loudly compete with each other, until the inevitable glaring scowl from the Sister lowered the volume automatically.

Once the service ended the occupants of each house filed out, behind their respective Sisters in pairs, towards the red-brick Brampton Hall adjoining the junior school, to take their positions at one of the long tables arranged in rows facing the stage, assigned for each individually named house.

Earlier tables had been decorated in a different Christmas theme, by a selected group competing for the "Governor's Best Table Award!" Included in the displays were angels, snowmen, miniature reindeer and sleighs, together with all the usual seasonal paraphernalia, such as holly and pinecones, carefully positioned on imitation cotton wool snow in the center of the table, extending the full length!

Following the judging and announcement of winners on stage by the Governor the long, eagerly anticipated moment arrived. Mr. Salt, the baker, now wearing his tall white chef's hat, entered with great ceremony carrying the first huge turkey aloft on a silver platter, followed closely by a line of culinary assistants similarly attired and loaded. The hall resounded with spontaneous cheers from hundreds of hungry throats and excited clapping ensued, as he lowered the first weighty tray on the center table and began to carve.

As each houses name was called the inhabitants stood and filed slowly past, to receive slices of turkey meat, stuffing, roasted potatoes and Brussels sprouts, positioned carefully on each outstretched plate. Thick, brown gravy was poured over the top from a long-handled cup-shaped ladle, making it without doubt the most eagerly awaited meal of the whole year, when even the usually inedible gray-green vegetables, now bright and crisp, were ravenously devoured. It always surprised me how well cooked, colorful and tasty the food was on this particular day and yet how rancid and unappetizing it was the remainder of the year, until eventually realizing that Mister Salt personally supervised the preparation of this annual festive repast.

Following the sumptuous Christmas dinner, a few previously selected members from each house contributed to an act on stage for everyone's entertainment, which included the full choir, soloists, dancers and gymnasts, all of whom displayed a remarkable variety of talents. Particularly enjoyable were the soloists, invariably accompanied by Sister Fanny, still remembered with much affection from my early days in the Nursery School. Watching her hands and arms bounce up and down above the keys, her be-wigged, ginger hair shaking in rhythm to the tune, reminded me of an earlier much happier period. Later, displaying an encouraging smile she expressed kind words of encouragement to the performers and her past ex-boarders.

Both my sisters who sang in the choir also participated in the Christmas staged productions, as did my fellow gymnast brother. During Audrey's solo vocal performance she frequently smiled, glancing in my direction, waiting at the edge of the stage for my turn to participate.

At one Christmas party during the war, boys from Meriden House put on a gymnastics demonstration dressed in brand new navy blue shorts and white singlet's, with rubber-soled plimsoles that actually fitted. Unfortunately all clothing had to be handed back after the show for safekeeping and other future performances. Our prowess was demonstrated on the vaulting horse, parallel bars and balancing beam, leaping and tumbling to great applause. For the finale a pyramid was formed with older, taller boys forming the base, while younger, lighter beings gradually clambered upwards athletically onto the shoulders of the boy immediately beneath them.

Invariably, being the smallest and lightest in the whole group, it was my lot to be nominated the final one to climb up and balance on the shoulders of the pair at the apex. A very precarious position to be in and one which often gave me great concern, looking down at the myriad of faces watching in awe from the numerous rows of tables, fortunately somehow always managing to descend without incident, even as the pyramid rhythmically swayed below me. This elevated demonstration would have been considerably much easier on an empty stomach, rather than having to participate during the personal bloated feeling resulting from such an unaccustomed feast.

When the annual party and entertainment finally concluded everyone returned to their respective houses, to spend the remainder of the day playing with their newly acquired possessions. For reasons unknown at the time, on this particular evening just before bedtime miserable homesickness overcame me, missing my mother and siblings more than at any other time. Tightly clutching the card and gift, in deep despair, desperately wishing they were present. What should have been the happiest day of the year became the saddest, never understanding why my sisters, or later even my brother, were not allowed to visit even on Christmas Day! Laying silently in the dark on this particular night I often cried myself to sleep, as the fantasy gradually faded, until awakening once again to harsh, cold reality.

Summer school holidays, on the other hand, which lasted for six weeks during July and August, were long and full of exciting escapades, many of which were the cause for inevitably ending up in trouble. Although looking back as a parent and grandparent, most of the mischief involving my participation would now probably be brushed off as a mere "boyishness"!

One particular day everyone looked forward to during the summer break was "Fete Day", when the grounds were thrown open to the public, parents and potential wealthy benefactors, invited to visit and observe the "day to day" running of the home. The large mowed-grass oval, in front of the red brick administrative building and church, was surrounded with a variety of decorated canvas-topped booths, manned by sisters and children from each individual house.

Knitted articles, sewn or hand made during the long winter

months, were displayed for sale together with appetizing baked goods, fresh fruit, flowers and vegetables from the home farm and gardens. Normally few of these were seldom seen, let alone enjoyed by the young residents.

In the center of The Oval, different games and races were organized between competing house teams, separately for boys and girls. They included three-legged races, sack races, running, jumping and apple bobbing, which was a favorite. Winners were rewarded with sweets and homemade toffee-dipped apples, making the rivalry very fierce, although everyone was on their best behavior, not just for the fun but also in anticipation of the edible, sugary prizes.

Strings of brightly colored triangular flags and banners fluttered above each stall and draped over the arched entrance to the church, which like all other buildings was open to visitors, after being cleaned meticulously by young church members during early morning chores.

There were some lucky children whose relatives actually visited on Fete Day, although none of ours were ever present on that particular occasion, even though I constantly dreamt of it. Every boy, however, was clothed meticulously, sporting a clean white, short-sleeved shirt, knitted woolen tie, knee-length socks and, if not competing in the games, given a responsible position at one of the numerous sideshows.

One particular stall I assisted at was located at the bottom of the clock tower steps, where most visitors entered the inner grounds. A large, square wicker laundry basket was positioned at the bottom of the steps, with the interior filled almost to overflowing with thousands of used postage stamps from all over the world. Every conceivable design and color, removed carefully from envelopes or packages delivered throughout the previous year, had been carefully deposited in the basket by a frugal secretary or staff member. Obviously the bulk of stamps came from England, showing either the head of King George the Fifth or his son George the Sixth, who succeeded to the throne after the scandalous abdication of his older brother Edward. A few stamps still bore the likeness of Queen Victoria, causing quite a stir among a few of the delving collectors.

As people rummaged down through the depths of the pile many brightly colored "foreign" stamps were also uncovered, each one giving a reason for much excitement. Unknown names and scenes, depicting distant places from throughout the Empire, created great interest and wide-eyed wonderment when offered up for sale at a penny-a-piece, attracting numerous buyers, obvious ardent collectors, hoping to discover a rare print for their albums. Differing value coins in payment were dropped into a thong-tied canvas bag held by one of the sisters, who kept a beady eye on us at the same time, ensuring nobody pocketed any. The one penny coins were probably those later handed out on to us each Sunday and dutifully deposited in the collection plate at church. To this day postage stamps from my own mail are still automatically saved, keeping them in a large envelope, before eventually passing them on to close family or friends who may also be amateur philatelists.

It was a tradition and a requirement during the summer holidays over a week or more, for young boys over seven to be sent down to the home farm to help the farmer pick vegetable crops. Never quite certain whether the practice of nominating certain individuals was considered a punishment for the badly behaved, or a privilege to be enjoyed. Either way it was a job each boy looked forward to, because it was outdoors and any activity outside in the summer sun was welcome. The hours were long and started very early in the morning after breakfast, lasting until dusk with a short lunch break at noon. Even the usual drudgery of early morning chores were foregone, for those having to traipse down the lane to work on the farm, which in itself was an incentive to be chosen.

In the fields, on command, each boy lined up facing a row of leafy potato plants at the far end, close to the farmhouse. Gradually working down each row in turn, the bulky plants were pulled out of the rich black soil by hand and new potatoes shaken into a round, thickly woven wicker basket. When completely full, it often became too heavy to lift, so two boys had to drag it by the thick rope handles across the uneven furrows to the edge of the field. Waiting patiently, one of the normally pastured workhorse friends stood hitched to a tall, wooden wheeled farm tumbrel. The basket was emptied over the slatted sides by two older farm hands, until filled to the brim, then hauled to nearby trenches where the potatoes were tipped out, covered with dry straw and thick black dirt forming high rounded mounds.

Back in the field, as each long furrow was stripped, another was immediately started, until finally the whole crop was harvested and deeply buried. Midday, lunch consisted of a hunk of freshly baked bread and cheese, with a mug of cool milk taken directly from the farm dairy, an unaccustomed treat, usually enjoyed sitting atop the huge, straw-covered earth hillocks engulfing the piles of newly picked potatoes.

In the beginning, crouching down for so long was back-breaking hard work and at the end of each day boys laboriously walked back up the lane to their respective houses, physically exhausted. Gradually however, over the course of a few days, by the time the whole crop was harvested we had become fitter and more used to the labor, even finding time to dawdle in the late afternoon, sitting on the sloping grassy banks lining the sides of the lane. A couple of us also took advantage of the unaccustomed freedom to flirt with home girls who may be in the vicinity, or explore the numerous nooks and crannies in other areas of the farm.

The type of crop to be pulled, including turnips, carrots, or even kale, determined the finishing time for each individual team. Mr. Hall the farmer, usually a good natured person, kept us all hard at work in the fields, but if the day's efforts ended early enough he often showed a few of us around the other farm operations. Cow barns, milking sheds, pigsties and horse stable were visited and described in detail, while afterwards we were allowed to help feed and clean the animals, or even operate the milk-pasteurizing machine, once again rewarded with a glass of fresh full-cream milk.

Pigs' feed, or "swill" as it was known, was cooked in a huge, round, cast-iron boiler, heated by a wood-burning fire underneath. One boy at a time had the job of stirring the steaming concoction with a large wooden ladle, whilst balancing atop a high raised platform. The mixture consisted of sliced vegetable ends from kale, cabbages, carrots and some of the freshly dug potatoes, not considered quite fresh enough to store. To a hungry boy the rancid smell was not unappetizing and frequently we carefully extracted a well-cooked potato from the boiling liquid and ravenously gobbled up the inside. The hot outer skin was stripped carefully and tossed back into the steaming cauldron. Similarly, tips of raw carrots, turnips and the soft white core of cabbage or kale were greedily devoured, before adding the left-over's to the mixture, without ever feeling we were denying the pigs, considering how fat and healthy they all looked. Working on the land most certainly provided us with an opportunity to supplement our customary meager, unappetizing diet and we took full advantage of it.

A plentiful supply of seasoned fruits also grew in abundance around the farm or in the garden nursery, and we were often tempted to climb the trees and steal apples, pears, plums, and black, sweet damsons. In the local dialect this practice was known as "scrumping," although I never made the connection. Perhaps it was something to do with the fruit being so scrumptious?

One day, when farm work was finished, two of us decided to climb one of the well laden damson trees, with the intent of filling our trouser pockets with the tempting juicy fruit. After a short while, with pockets bulging, we carefully climbed the nearby open-sided hay barn, using the long pointed, wooden locking shafts protruding from the sides as a ladder. The shafts, or spears, were thrust deep into the hay at regular intervals to hold bales together and prevent them from falling, but they also made an ideal ladder for small boys to climb up.

Upon reaching the top we settled down in the limited space between the oblong bales and corrugated metal roof to spread out our "ill-gotten gains." Before long we had greedily disposed of each damson, playfully spitting the stones over the edge of the stack to the hard ground, totally unconcerned.

Suddenly a stern voice from below demanded; "Who is up there?"
"I can hear you! Come on down!"

Recognizing the man's voice, we desperately scrambled deeper between the soft hay bales, crouching silent, hardly daring to breathe.

"If you don't' come down, I'm coming up!"

There was a pause, then grunting and heavy breathing as the farmer attempted to climb, presumably the same way we had but unfortunately, of course, he was much heavier! Crack! A shaft broke then another, as his weight bore down. There came a curse, a muffled grunt and the sound of a heavy body hitting the ground. We stared, wide-eyed at each other, covering our mouths trying not to laugh.

"I'll be back with a ladder!" he shouted angrily, hobbling away down the lane.

Nervously crawling across the bales on our stomachs, we peered over the edge and watched him slowly making his way toward the farm buildings, his large rubber Wellington Boots squelching in the mud. Once he disappeared out of sight, we frantically scrambled over the bales, grappling our way down the far side, out of view, back to the ground. At full speed taking off running as fast as stubby legs could, along the high, hedge-lined sunken lane, to the comparative safety of the long grassy meadow behind the hospital. Eventually we ended up safe but breathless back at Meriden House. For some time after this incident I felt guilty whenever I saw the farmer in church or passed him by, feeling certain he knew who the trespassers had been in the hay-barn.

During the night, however, both of us were punished in kind for our escapade, in the form of a violent tummy-ache, obviously caused by an over-indulgence of fruit. Inevitably the result was a headlong dash in the dark to the downstairs toilet, to sit doubled-up, painfully contemplating the wisdom of our earlier actions. On the way back to the bedroom passing my friend on his way down, also obviously suffering a similar fate.

Many years later, after leaving The Orphanage, we discovered the farmer actually paid for each boy conscripted to work in the fields, but during my stay I certainly never received any form of payment. Not until eventually managing to return home, did my mother surprisingly receive a check for wages earned at the farm the previous summer.

The home farm held many happy memories for me, in particular my introduction to the heavy work horses that pulled the plough and milk cart, or were periodically pastured to rest in the meadow behind the hospital. Endless long summer hours were spent in their quiet company, lounging in the tall wavy grass among numerous wild flowers, watching them graze. Occasionally lying across their broad backs, until eventually they allowed me to ride astride as they meandered across the field. It became an early and long lasting relationship, enjoyed for decades and to this day, with the magnificently patient equine.

Late in the spring of 1944, at the age of twelve, the countryside appeared much quieter than previously, at least in the skies above where enemy bombers had earlier flown causing a frantic scurry to shelters. Only the drone of a single engine airplane from a cloudless blue sky, now occasionally interrupted the birds and bees.

On the roads and rails however, late into the evenings there was a great deal of activity, particularly from the American and British soldiers still stationed in Sutton Park. Every day a seemingly endless convoy of trucks drove noisily past heading southwards, carrying helmeted soldiers laden with large packs and a variety of weapons. Waving and shouting they threw out packets of gum or chocolate bars, hurriedly scrambled for, while larger, canvas-topped trucks towed heavy, long-barreled, wheeled guns, or long flat trailers carried armored cars or huge, iron-tracked tanks.

Suddenly it had become quiet again with only a few local vehicles passing, apparently nearly everyone, except the prisoners of war, had left the park and even the shops and streets were no longer crowded with uniformed servicemen. Early in the summer the Prime Minister Winston Churchill made a speech, relayed over the Sisters' sitting room radio one night and overheard from my usual punishment position, on the flat Hessian mat, behind the door under the playroom bench. The official announcement stated that, on June sixth, the combined D-Day landings on the Normandy Beaches by the Allied Forces had begun, which gave credence to earlier suppositions. However, unknown to us at the time, the invasion marked the eventual end of the war. Over the continuing long summer I was personally to experience both extreme happiness and bitter disappointment, completely separate from the on-going fluctuating news of the allied troop movements in Europe.

The lessening of the war threat meant that the populace was once again allowed to go about their usual daily routines. Travel restrictions were lifted and people were able to visit relatives and friends, who perhaps they may not have seen since the start of hostilities. One day my sister Audrey received a letter from our mother, containing the good news that finally it was possible for her and our two elder sisters, Yvonne and Joan, to visit us, making the one hundred mile train journey north from London. The news caused great excitement among the four of us and personally I went out of my way to be on my very best behavior for weeks before the scheduled date, for fear of being "indisposed" on the special day! A frequently repeated threat, once a relative had announced a visit was, "You had better be good, or else," containing very obvious implications.

In her letter Mum described in detail how they were planning to travel by train to Birmingham New Street station and then by "Midland Red" bus, stopping at the corner of Jockey and Chester Road, opposite the austere Catholic Convent. We all knew the location well as it was just a short walk from the home, so arrangements were made to meet there. At the appointed time on Saturday, standing grouped together, we anxiously waited for what seemed an endless time, as bus after bus drew up at the stop and drove on without recognizing anyone stepping off. Anxiously scanning the windows on both the lower and upper decks, we watched carefully as passengers descended from inside and down the spiral staircase at the rear, uncertain whether we would know her after such a long absence. Eventually, just as we were about to give up hope, a beautiful lady in a broad-brimmed hat and high fur-collared coat stepped out onto the rear platform, smiling and waving. Instinctively we rushed forward, anxious to have the first hug, feel the softness of her touch and inhale the almost forgotten perfume that pervaded my senses, while clinging eagerly to her delicately gloved hand.

Accompanying her were our two eldest sisters, Yvonne and Joan and a tall, middle-aged gentleman, wearing a long, knee-length tweed overcoat and broad-brimmed trilby hat. He was introduced to us as "Uncle Arthur," a name never heard before, but later we discovered he was not actually a real uncle, but "a close friend of the family who lived nearby"!

Shortly following the reunion we returned to The Orphanage, to inform the head sister our mother was visiting and we were all being taken out for the day. Mum had some difficulty convincing Sister Nellie to allow us to wear socks with sandals, insisting proper attire was required for travelling around the big city. Sister Nellie maintained socks were usually only worn on the Sabbath, however, eventually and begrudgingly she gave in and we all set off for a day out in the big city correctly dressed. The one thing always hated about wearing long socks were the broad elastic garters, worn under the top fold to prevent them slipping down. Invariably the elastic was so tight it left deep red weals around the upper calves, itching constantly and restricting circulation, so most boys pushed the tops down to their ankles to relieve the pressure. This action invariably brought about a strong physical rebuke from the Head Sister, particularly if attempted prior to entering the church for Sunday morning service.

On this first visit to the City of Birmingham, since arriving as an infant almost nine years earlier, the outward appearance had not changed much, except for numerous bombed out, derelict buildings; grimy, gray and smelling of smoke. With so much unaccustomed traffic noise and pedestrian bustle I desperately clutched Mum's gloved hand, as we wove our way along the overcrowded pavements.

In one huge department store we were treated to a full English Tea at the "posh" restaurant, sitting at a round table with a crocheted, lace-edged cloth and silver knives and forks. Little triangular cucumber sandwiches, cut so thin you could almost see through them were served, with tiny jam tarts and iced cakes so scrumptious we couldn't stop eating. Afterwards we toured the store and "Uncle Arthur" bought both Maurice and me gifts of our own choosing, making me vaguely wonder why Audrey and Pauline weren't also asked. My individual choice, however, was an elegant, sleek wooden sailboat, with a bright blue painted hull and white canvas sails suspended from the mast and boom by string rigging. I had earlier mentioned to Mum my desire to own one, after learning from my eldest sister Yvonne that an earlier ancestor had once been a mariner, naturally an opportunity to sail it on the nearby lake in Sutton Park was eagerly anticipated.

After returning to Meriden House, Mum, an accomplished pianist with a wonderful singing voice, sat down at the ancient upright piano in the playroom, persuaded by Audrey and Pauline to play for us. Unfortunately, at that time we learned she could only play from sheet music. Under pressure from us all however, Mum eventually played and sung the one piece she knew by ear "Home Sweet Home." We all, of course, were very aware there really was "no place like home" and that particular close family moment eventually became, for me, a very sad time to remember.

Later during the afternoon, while spending a few hours together on the front lawn, we played on the swings where photographs were taken with a little black Kodak box camera held by "Uncle Arthur". It was such a beautiful warm sunny day and one never wanting to end, but inevitably and eventually the dreaded time came when we all pleaded with Mum, desperate to know when we would finally be going home. Sitting as a family group in front of the church we were told that it would not be possible for us all to go home "at the present time," but only Audrey and Pauline would be accompanying Mum and Arthur on the train back to London, later that evening." Unfortunately", Mum quietly added, both Maurice and I would have to stay "just a little while longer."

Suddenly, realizing the reason earlier gifts had been bought only for the two of us, I became utterly devastated. At that moment hating everyone, not only because we were now condemned to stay in such a horrible place even longer, but were also being deprived the company of our sisters! It was bad enough having to earlier suffer individual segregation into separate houses, but now also being denied the occasional comfort and support given by Audrey and Pauline, albeit on rarely allowed occasions, was unthinkable and utterly unbearable! "It won't be for too much longer," we were sympathetically told, although, in fact, confinement dragged on for another full year for me, before the promise became reality due to my own desperate actions, and even longer for Maurice!

That evening, after tearful good-byes to my mother and sisters, sitting alone on the wooden playroom floor in Meriden House, sobbing and feeling totally neglected, the toy sailboat lying in front of me I questioned, "When will I ever get to sail it?"

Desperately, no longer wanting it, grabbing the tall masts I angrily flung it across the room, smashing the sleek hull against the solid wooden lockers. Miserable, dejected and frustrated I ran over and stamped on it repeatedly with both feet until it broke into multiple pieces, enmeshed in string and tattered canvas. Leaving the pile of debris on the floor, dashing out of the playroom running up stairs, I threw myself convulsively gasping onto the iron-framed bed, feeling pathetically alone and forgotten, as on numerous previous occasions eventually crying myself to sleep.

Early next morning, for the first time a plan to run away was conceived, determined not to stay in that horrible place any longer, by whatever means possible I was going to find my way home. It would, however, prove to be some considerable time before being able to succeed permanently. For many weeks after their visit pathetically walking down to the nearby bus stop on Saturdays, in the vain hope Mum would once again step off. Patiently standing for hours while bus after bus went by, before eventually having to give up and despondently return back to my doleful existence.

As fate would have it, very good news was later received that I would actually be going home for a whole week's holiday during the summer. Apparently other family members, after hearing how disappointed we were, offered to have just one of us stay with them. Unfortunately for Maurice he had to wait for "another time," which, in fact, turned out to be a very long time coming.

The semi-detached, two bed-roomed rented home in Romford, had become a little crowded now with four girls, so my favorite Aunt Doris, Mums older sister, with Uncle Percy had made the offer. Their sons, Tony and Dennis, both of whom were older than I, attended a prestigious grammar school in the neighboring town of Ilford, located closer to the City of London. At a certain point a few miles east of London the main highway divided onto London Road, heading towards Romford and Eastern Avenue leading from Ilford towards Epping Forest, a nearby picturesque local "Green Belt" and wild deer forest preserve.

My Aunts home with the name "Sunninghill" on a little chrome plate attached to the front gate was located on Eastern Avenue, separated back from the road by a wide grass-verged footpath. Their home was much larger than the house my Mother rented and boasted a spacious fenced garden at the rear containing open flowerbeds, with a large front lawn protected from the pedestrian pavement by a low brick wall.

A short distance away a beautiful laid out area known as Cranbrook Park boasted two lakes, one where children sailed toy model yachts and the other where adults rented dark polished, wooden rowing boats with flat bottoms and ornamental, cast iron high backed seats. On long summer afternoons fashionably dressed ladies lounged beneath parasols, while blazer-bedecked gentlemen rowed strenuously from a low, wooden seat in the center. During the all-to-brief holiday many hours were enjoyed sailing my cousin's model yacht and being taught to row by Dennis in the tranquil surroundings. I actually regretted destroying the new toy sailboat earlier during my childish temper tantrum, which became a secret kept from my mother for many years.

Uncle Percy, who owned a greengrocer shop in town, was considered quite well off, particularly as he owned a brand new highly polished motorcar, a possession not enjoyed by many families during the war. Sitting at his side in the front passenger seat, my real Uncle drove me the few miles across country to see Mum and my sisters a couple of times throughout the week long holiday, where surprisingly I was to meet the new "Uncle Arthur" once again.

Unfortunately, being so excited at going home and enthralled with the unaccustomed luxury of the car journey, the thought never occurred to remember the route to the house in Romford. Although every other stage of the train and road journey to The Orphanage in Birmingham had become engraved in my memory, without realizing how useful such stored knowledge would be in the very near future. The eventual end of a wonderful exciting week came all too soon and despite tearful pleadings to stay, I was once more transported back to the Midlands and the dismal confines of the "Children's Home" for another undetermined lengthy continuance.

Such was my state of anxiety at the time, up to this day there is no recollection of how the return journey was made or with whom. For a long time afterwards wondering why it was not possible for both or either one of us, to live with any one of a number of close relatives. In addition to Auntie Doris and Uncle Percy, there were three or four other relatives with only a single child who lived within a reasonable distance, who could perhaps have helped. For whatever reason, however, nobody ever offered to take any of us in after Father died and the subject was never fervently pursued with either Mum or any of them. Years later however, until fate intervened, I enjoyed very good relationships with most nearby family members lasting well into the future.

10

Isolation

The most frequently prescribed form of punishment regardless of the misdemeanor was to be sent up to stay alone in the bedroom, which was, of course, preferable to the more physical abuse metered out by certain staff members. "Out of sight, out of mind" was probably the reasoning behind the decision. The length of banishment invariably hinged on the seriousness of the offense and could last a few hours or in some instances all day. Depending on the whim of the Sister on duty and the length of her memory determined how long you stayed, or whether any meals were sent up. If they were it was usually another boy designated to take up a tray, invariably proving beneficial to a lonely detainee, particularly if it was a friend who could smuggle items such as paper, pencils or small playthings. Often it became a habit to peer around the doorpost, looking down the long wooden staircase to the dingy hallway below, hoping to catch a glimpse of a sympathetic fellow passing.

Messages were sometimes carried back and forth describing who was currently on duty and the kind of "atmosphere" downstairs, particularly if Sister Nellie forgot about the boy upstairs before leaving on an urgent errand, a not uncommon occurrence! Her assistant Sister Eva, on the other hand, was more sympathetic towards ending the punishment earlier, especially if reminded by one's friend that a boy was still confined upstairs. Generally, however, once sent up you stayed there for as long as the Head Sister decreed, or remembered.

A common, ongoing reason for doling out any kind of punishment was known as "Dumb Insolence;" a personal descriptive term the sisters used regarding any involuntary facial expression which may appear when reacting to an abusive oral comment, or threat of physical punishment. In my case the look was often instinctively one of sheer defiance, disgust or disappointment at my own predicament.

Left alone for such long periods in an empty room, created boredom, extreme loneliness and anxieties, which inevitably developed into feelings of inadequacy and frustration, causing me to become a very private person and somewhat a loner well into adulthood.

If more than one boy was being punished seclusion became infinitely more bearable, because two boys were able to play games together like, "I spy," "Charades" or "Noughts and Crosses," to while-away the time. Even if one had been sent to a separate room, frequently the case, it was still possible to sneak along the adjoining landing, if the coast was clear, to meet up. Obviously this was very risky and if caught the culprit would suffer even more punishment, usually by the vicious flaying of a rubber soled gym shoe wielded at arms length across a naked posterior.

At first, if sent up for short periods at weekends, one was usually allowed to remain dressed in day clothes, though not permitted to get under the bed covers but only sit on the edge. Boots had to be removed and left downstairs in the individual cubbyholes in the Boot Room. Later, however, when it was discovered naughty boys didn't always stay put, clothes were also confiscated and only nightshirts were allowed to be worn until the isolation period ended, although offenders were still not permitted to actually get into bed. When temperatures became particularly low, general practice was to slip under the top bedspread until someone was heard coming up the stairs, then at the first creaking sound leap out, smooth the covers and sit innocently on the edge, never quite certain whether the pretence of having been in the same position had been detected or not! Isolated in this manner time dragged by infinitely slowly, so to ward off depression some quite inventive and imaginative pastimes were developed, including many passed on from previously confined boys.

If lucky enough to retain clothes, the contents of trouser pockets often provided many interesting items to preoccupy your attention for the duration of the stay. Colored glass marbles, five stones, or "jacks" as they were known, little toy lead soldiers, Dinky Toys, a length of string or even an odd shaped piece of wood provided hours of entertainment.

There were boys who actually owned a penknife or even a pet white mouse, forbidden of course, probably because they frightened the Sisters, although a large variety of items were always being swapped around, so there were quite a number either individually owned or "borrowed".

At the far end of the bedroom an old brick-framed fireplace was boarded up and strange noises often emitted from behind the planked-wood cover, giving rise to all kinds of ghostly stories, gleefully related to younger more impressionable boys at night. Squat, cast iron radiators set under the window ledges provided little if any heat and most of the time the room was draughty and cold, particularly when the door to the landing was closed, shutting out what little heat arose from downstairs.

Five stones, usually carried in a trouser pocket, were real white, flat little stones, carefully picked for shape and size, doubling as flint stones because when struck sharply together they produced bright sparks. Great fun was had beneath a hurriedly erected tent-like sheet at night, creating brilliant flashes without realizing the fire risk we were taking under the dry, fibrous material. Much later during my military career I was reminded of this boyish incident by the smell of explosive cordite on the firing range.

Manufactured, star-shaped variety of five stones were made of gray gunmetal and sold in local toyshops, unaffordable to us, of course, hence the substitution, although actually the game remained the same whatever type was used. Four of the "stones" were thrown indiscriminately onto a flat surface, whilst retaining a single one in the palm of the hand, then an attempt was made to pick up one at a time, while tossing a second in the air trying to catch it. The main objective was to eventually balance all five on the back of one hand, not an easy exercise unless you were individually ambidextrous. Many boys became quite proficient, particularly those individuals who were forced to spend lengthy periods of time in solitude.

"Dinky Toys," the forerunner of "Matchbox Toys," were highly sought after miniature models of cars and trucks of the era. Even during the war, toy factories that had yet to convert to munitions still produced miniature camouflaged armored vehicles, aero planes and leaden soldiers. With extremely limited amounts of pocket-money to spend extra toys were very difficult to obtain. Somehow we managed by bartering or other devious means to acquire them, usually from "outside" boys who also attended the Secondary Modern School and whose parents were capable of affording the little "luxuries of life." Some privileged home-friends swore they had "found" a model, although I personally remember once owning an armored car, swapped for a piece of bomb shrapnel, found in a crater after one night time air raid. There was always something we "orphaned urchins" managed to acquire, which could be exchanged for expensive shop-bought items, owned by more well-to-do boys from local private homes. At one time, my personal collection included a variety of military vehicles, ships and even a double-decker, "Midland Red" bus, any of which could be stuffed into either trouser-pocket at some time.

The thin cotton, paisley bedspread, covering the single red blanket on top of the bed, bore curled white line patterns woven into the pale red base. When bedclothes were rumpled or bunched up, they resembled hills and valleys. The intricate lines represented narrow, twisting roads weaving through, making it a perfect landscape for playing "war games" or simulating a village or town scene. Left on my own I became absorbed for many hours pushing toy vehicles along imaginary roads, setting up an ambush with the lead soldiers, or just pretending to drive home or travel to some far distant land.

On rare occasions there may not have been anything in my pocket except a piece of dry wood or string, but even these items were made into playthings to help while-away the long, lonely time. A popular game at the time, particularly with girls, as described by my sister Pauline, was to make a string cradle using both hands. A partner was required as the game progressed for passing the string from one person to the other, and although an attempt was made to use my feet it did not work, unfortunately.

Those lucky enough to own a pocketknife spent the time whittling, carving or gouging initials or crude hieroglyphics on wooden window ledges or even lead fascia outside each window. I often wonder today upon hearing lawyers clambering to sue on behalf of people affected by lead or asbestos poisoning, as we were continually in contact with both.

When windows were opened for air during the summer, similar markings were frequently gouged into the red clay-brick frame. Many years after leaving The Princess Alice Orphanage, during the period of my sole return visit, numerous initials, including mine, were still visible and remained there presumably until the eventual demolition of all the homes. Without these personal items, particularly when day clothes were removed, time dragged by and a great deal of time was spent standing on the edge of the bed or balancing precariously on the wainscoting, or window ledge, watching other children playing games happily on the broad grass oval below.

In spite of never actually owning a white mouse, as did a friend, I became quite skilled at catching various other indoor pests inhabiting the room, including shiny black, hard-backed beetles, spiders and even sun-dozy flies that fell victim to my stealthy stalking. The little black beetles were poked or prodded behind to race two at a time along a worn plank on the floor, while de-winged flies were placed skillfully in the center of a spider's web. Observing the spider's speedy, silken mummifying ritual attack often provided lengthy educational and amusing entertainment.

During earlier lonely periods of banishment my ability to mentally shut out depressing surroundings and conjure up fantasies about all manner of situations was discovered. Visualizing visits from my mother on bright sunny days or transporting myself back home, attended by older sisters in the garden or romping in nearby Hainault Forest among the bracken and wild flowers enabling me to completely close my mind off from reality. Only to be brought back from my daydreams, when shaken by a frustrated House Sister into sudden cruel awareness. For brief periods managing to escape the monotonous existence and gather strength from the knowledge that one day my fantasies would become real.

A short while after one period of isolation, my sister, Pauline, de-scribed an incident to me involving one of her personal fantasies which actually materialized. Following a minor misdemeanor, which had apparently annoyed the sister in charge, Pauline was ordered to her dormitory to stay in isolation, obviously a form of punishment also common in the girl's houses. On the way up stairs Pauline commented to the sister; "I won't be here for very long because my Mum is coming to see me today and you will have to fetch me down."

This was a fantasy all inmates had visualized at some time, but on this particular day, it came true! By coincidence our Mother did actu-ally visit the home that day much too every ones surprise, including Sister Flora Ruck, who embarrassingly had to break the news. Somehow Pauline had remained firmly convinced it was going to happen anyway.

Lying alone for hours, staring at the ceiling, it was destined to be only a matter of time before beginning to experience feelings, common to all virile teenage males with a vivid imagination, which soon led to an awareness of my masculinity and lack of inhibitions. I do not recall the exact time the practice began but the circumstances of my confine-ment certainly brought the acquired act of "self eroticism" to a head, so to speak, much sooner. At such an immature age not familiar with the common word for the indulgence, but it certainly helped pass the time more pleasurably on a number of occasions. At the time completely unaware whether or not it was an acceptable form of self-gratification I may have been perhaps punished even further if caught by the sister, but fortunately never was. Later the realization came that at night, listening in the dark, there were also a number of other boys in the bedroom who regularly participated in the energizing hand ritual.

On one particular Saturday morning, after being sent to stay in the bedroom for talking out of turn at the breakfast table, clothes were removed and after what seemed a particularly long, boring period of time left alone I decided to attempt an escape, even though attired solely in a long, knee-length linen nightgown.

Outside the open window of the dormitory a low brick parapet extended along the front of the building, with a shallow lead lined gutter trapping the rainwater from the gray-slated roof, directing it to a cast iron downspout extending to the ground. Leaning out over the high chamfered wooden window sill it appeared possible to clamber onto the parapet, without being seen from below.

Pausing to catch my breath before attempting to climb down and peer over the edge, I concluded that what at first appeared to be a comparatively easy descent from the window now seemed a very hazardous undertaking. The pipe which originally seemed to lie close to the low wall actually curved away, almost out of reach. None-the-less, by stretching my arms to the fullest extent it was possible to roll over and lower myself to straddle the pipe, wrapping my bare legs around it.

Suddenly there came a shout from below!

"Hey, look! Someone is up there!"

With great difficulty I turned to see two boys pointing up and laughing, obviously at the sight of my predicament and my bare posterior now exposed to all below. Desperately scrambling back up the pipe to the comparative safety and privacy behind the parapet, I hurriedly crawled along the edge around the corner to find another downspout. After a few moments crouching behind the low wall, I tentatively raised my head to look over again between the two houses, only to observe an even larger group of boys suddenly come into view running around the corner.

"There he is"! A boy shouted.

Hastily retreating once more, crawling on hands and knees gingerly back towards the open window, the decision was made to give up on my futile descent. At that precise moment Sister Nellie appeared at the open bedroom window, obviously attracted by the noise from below.

"Get in here you horrible boy, at once!" she demanded.

Knowing most certainly what the punishment would be if obeyed I squatted defiantly back down, realizing that, with such a bulky frame and lack of physical ability, the chances of her actually managing to struggle out of the window and reach me were obviously impractical, if not impossible.

The sloping slate roof extended down to the edge of the low wall where I still crouched, so there really was no other choice than to try and make it to the other side of the house by climbing up over the ridge, realizing the brick parapet did not extend around the side.

It was extremely difficult attempting to climb the slippery wet tiles on hands and knees, especially when bare toes kept catching inside the hem of my nightshirt. Eventually, however, managing to reach the apex of the roof and sit astride the curved tiles, clinging with both arms to the square brick chimney turrets as loud cheers came from the gathered throng below. Waving cheerily in response, mindful of the sudden notoriety, I almost lost my balance. Looking down the far side toward the back of the house, the incline appeared much steeper than previously ascended, causing me to panic and suddenly become affected by vertigo. Clinging even more desperately to the rough bricks, I attempted to not only maintain balance but also preserve my half naked dignity.

Gradually a steady drizzle began to seep through my flimsy, threadbare nightgown, causing violent shivering. By now an even larger crowd had gathered below, including boys, girls and members of staff, all looking up at my body perched precariously straddling the ridge in the falling rain. Summoning up courage and turning onto my stomach, grabbing for the slate tiles with outstretched hands, I slid backwards with ever increasing momentum to the relative safety of the brick parapet. The low wall fortunately broke my fall, ending up where previously begun, in a shallow puddle of rainwater floundering on my back.

"Come here, boy!" The deep rasping voice of Mr. Brassington was instantly recognizable, bellowing from the bedroom window, with his jacketed arm and hand outstretched. Reluctantly, fearing to disobey and trembling uncontrollably with the cold, slowly and submissively I crawled back along the narrow ledge towards him, head bowed, surrendering to the inevitable. Reaching out, grasping the massive hairy-backed paw which clamped over mine, my saturated, skinny frame was unceremoniously hauled back over the windowsill to flop saturated onto the inside floor. "Leave this to me, Sister," he commanded Sister Nellie, who still knowingly hovered nearby, but obediently left the room.

Slowly, deliberately walking back across the room after closing the door behind her, he turned toward me slapping the traditional long, black rubber soled gym shoe against his thigh. "Bend over, boy," he commanded.

Words frequently heard before hissed out of his tightly clamped lips, as my head was forced down over the iron foot rail of the bed, pressed into the sparsely covered horsehair mattress, while the back hem of the nightshirt was raised above my waist. The thin rubber shoe swished through the air just before stinging swipes landed across my exposed bottom causing a sudden wince, clenching my fingers deep into the bedclothes as welts begin to swell across tender skin. Finally, beating over, one ear was grabbed viciously between thumb and thick, pudgy index finger, dragging me protesting out of the bedroom and up the short flight of stairs to the top floor landing.

"Let me see you climb out of here!" he threatened, glaring through black, bushy eyebrows, while pushing my scantily clad, damp body through the narrow doorway into the small, sparsely furnished little room.

ISOLATION

Normally used for airing or ironing clothes and occasionally reserved for boys with a contagious illness, like Chicken Pox or Scarlet Fever, it was known as the Airing Room. Most boys however, referred to it as the Isolation Room because of its frequent use as a place for individual secluded punishment. As the door slammed shut behind me and the key turned in the solid, cast iron lock, eyes brimming with tears I gathered the wet nightshirt around my aching body and climbed painfully onto the top of the twin iron bunk bed set against the back wall. The bare room smelled of a mixture of carbolic, antiseptic and mothballs, combined with the familiar stench of a thin, urine-stained, horse-hair mattress, reminiscent of earlier days spent huddled beneath the playroom bench. Placed beside the bed was a three-legged, high wooden stool and on the far wall a narrow cupboard contained a metal-framed, padded ironing board propped beneath a shelf. Opposite, a small, high window had iron bars set inside the main frame with narrow spaces, which later I discovered were too narrow for my head to fit between. However, it was possible to peer out by turning to one side, enabling me with difficulty to see along the narrow footpath separating the houses, leading to the grass oval in front. Estimating the time to have been close to midday when locked in the room a meal was anticipated but none came, so the remainder of the afternoon was spent wondering if any food would ever be forthcoming. With the normally sparse breakfast meal so drastically interrupted earlier, pangs of hunger soon returned with a vengeance.

Time dragged infinitely slowly by with nothing to amuse me, except an occasional glimpse of a boy on the footpath, but it was impossible to get anyone's attention, even if they looked up it would have been very difficult to see my face at the small, barred upstairs window.

When it began to rain again I morosely traced the droplets running down the outside of the glass with an index finger, marking the inside condensation with intricately traced patterns. Utterly miserable and cold a sudden need to relieve myself developed. Fortunately there was the usual large, white porcelain chamber pot, half hidden under the bottom bunk, so slowly sliding it out, noticeably empty for once, I hurriedly and desperately expelled.

Climbing back onto the wire-sprung mattress frame, covering myself with the single red blanket, I buried my head tearfully into the un-cased striped pillow. Even the cold-damp nightshirt did nothing to ease my backside, still throbbing from the punishing painful red welts All this resulting primarily, from earlier speaking out of turn at the breakfast table and breaking the "silence at meals" rule.

For what seemed like hours, laying motionless staring up at the yellow stained plaster, picking out imaginary scenes and faces from the numerous cracks crisscrossing the flaky ceiling, finally as the evening shadows drifted across the window, the sound of a key turning in the lock preceded Sister Nellie bustling in.

"I hope you've learnt your lesson?

"Go to your room and get dressed!" she directed. "Then go down for your supper!"

Hurriedly squeezing past her and running down the top flight of stairs to the bedroom, where my clothes had been neatly placed on the bottom of the bed, grateful that by this time the flimsy nightshirt covering me had finally dried sufficiently to be awkwardly creased and folded back under the pillow.

The meager supper in the dining hall did nothing to replace two earlier missed meals, consisting only of the usual mug of lukewarm, grayish watery cocoa with a stale, whole-meal biscuit, slowly and deliberately nibbled around the edge to make it last longer. Luckily a sympathetic friend, completing a turn of duty at the urn, unobtrusively passed me an extra biscuit out of sight of "Billy Bunter," somewhat alleviating hunger pangs at least for a while.

This particularly lengthy afternoon spent in isolation was not, unfortunately, the first or the last to be endured, future similarly lonely and miserable experiences were to make me even more determined to somehow, one day, eventually find my way back home.

11

Running Away

The thought of running away from The Orphanage had been uppermost in my mind for some time, but how, when and where frequently troubled me. It had been discussed numerous times with my brother and a friend Johnny Butterworth, who had shared many little escapades in the past and offered to join me whenever an eventual decision was made. The idea of actually attempting to enlist and go off to war like many other local young men had also crossed our minds, but we were both obviously too young and quite small for our ages. Later in life, however, I was eventually recruited and became a "boy soldier" at the young age of fourteen although at the time my weight was a mere seventy nine pounds, at a height of only four and a half feet.

Anywhere or anyplace, was considered much better than where we were currently experiencing life. The chance to escape the daily abusive routine of the home, and the incessant religious indoctrination in church, provided a strong incentive for even considering such a dangerous and drastic step. Having previously attempted to hide a couple of times in different locations without actually leaving the orphanage grounds, I had realized that by teatime, after missing the mid-day meal, hunger forced me to return and, of course, suffer the consequences for my absence and the inevitable search by staff.

In the past there had been others who had tried and failed for various reasons, only to return and face severe punishment. Over time rumors circulated and were enlarged upon describing both incidents and punishments, to the point where culprits became almost revered as young heroes, although never emulated until the present, for fear of severe retribution. The plan to get away, however, was constantly present, particularly when we regularly mingled with locally resident boys at school, who obviously enjoyed a much easier life and infinitely more freedom than us.

Even in wartime, boys who lived outside the home but visited as members of soccer or sports teams at weekends, described family activities and lifestyles obviously far less restrictive and inhibitive than ours. Naturally we became resentful and jealous to the point where, in school particularly, confrontations occurred frequently over trivial little possessions or certain home privileges accepted as normal in a complete family. Many instances are recalled of personally being very envious of other boys' clothes, belongings, visits with relatives or trips to the country and even the contents of school satchels, particularly if they contained succulent items such as unaccustomed home baked pastries or cakes. Situations were made even worse when we were ridiculed or picked on by local bullies, who delighted in making fun of our hand-me-down, worn clothing. Patches sewn onto the seats of our short serge trousers and elbows of jackets caused regular abuse and inevitable fights. Fortunately we invariably became victors, probably due to being physically leaner, meaner and backed up by each other in any conflict with outsiders.

On rare occasions when not engaged in fights with the Kingstanding Town locals, or participating in home sports we usually walked to the nearby park, a natural expanse of woods, lakes and rolling gorse-covered hills officially listed as "Green Belt," or Nature Preserve. Known locally as Sutton Park it was described earlier in the chapter on "The War". At this particular moment in time very little of the environmental damage, caused by Allied Forces to such natural beauty, had been repaired.

In making our first joint decision to run away, the park was chosen as the initial get-away location for a number of reasons. Within the grounds picnicking areas were laid out with wooden tables and benches, plus fresh drinking water fountains conveniently positioned with long, metal pump-type handles on one side. Close to the sheltering woods in an open area, a large shallow lake, dotted by patches of water lilies, was often used as a swimming or paddling pool. Earlier, during the war, a submerged broken coke bottle, obviously discarded by an allied serviceman, had almost severed my big toe. At the main entrance between two square, hard-wood pillars, black wrought-iron gates had once swung, removed at the start of the war for smelting down into munitions and replaced by thick solid oak designs.

A short walking distance inside, extending along the edge of the black tarmac road, a large acreage of trees included mature Oaks, Horse Chestnuts, Elms and many other forms of tall foliage, thickly intermingled with grass scrub and saplings. Every autumn the floor of the Forest was carpeted with masses of fallen leaves and broken twigs, covering rapidly fading green areas, while in the spring a huge carpet of bluebells, daffodils and numerous wild flowers formed a colorful canopy. Short, thick bushes and shrubs protected many hidden areas among the tree roots, often used for hide-and-seek or for making dens. Should one wandered off the narrow beaten pathways it was easy to get lost or disoriented, unless you knew the area well, making these secret locations an ideal safe place to hide or shelter.

During numerous visits, both supervised and unaccompanied, I became very familiar with the layout of the park, obviously giving me a feeling of complete confidence in my ability to stay there undetected for an indefinite period. Earlier, while playing in one particularly well sheltered part of the woods, a friend and I had discovered a large dense bush covering a cave-like opening. Inside, a sloping soft moss-covered bank nestled between the roots of a massive sheltering Horse Chestnut tree. With very little effort we managed to disguise the opening further with bracken and leafy branches. From there, we surmised, we could possibly venture out for food and water during the day and be comfortably secure from creatures at night. Initially I believe we had visions of a kind of "Tarzan of the Jungle" existence or Robin Hood in Sherwood Forest. Both films were very popular at the time for Saturday morning matinees in local cinemas

Over a short period we managed to procure and smuggle out from the scout hut various items thought to prove useful, including a couple of "Dixie Cans," water bottles, two enamel mugs and an old canvas groundsheet, proving that previous Boy Scout training was finally to be put to the ultimate test. Inside the small den there was just enough room for the two of us to lay down in reasonable comfort, completely out of sight from any passer-by. Discovery would be doubtful anyway, because by climbing into the upper branches of the giant tree, anyone approaching from a distance could easily be spotted.

Later that summer, together with my friend John Butterworth, we chose one Saturday afternoon for our first serious attempt at running away. Timing was important because during the afternoon we were allowed out for only a few hours to play, if not participating in a pre-arranged sport, before having to return for the ritual teatime. At this time both of us owned a small, canvas scout rucksack, which was packed with some spare clothes and other items, including a spare pair of sandals, tied on the outside and a small amount hastily snaffled food. The previous day my current "girlfriend" had baked some savory pastries in her school "home economics" class, hurriedly stuffed in my pack together with a couple of apples and a few broken biscuits, stolen earlier from the barrelful outside the local tuck shop.

Eventually retrieving the packs from one of the lower shelves in the boot room, where they lay hidden, we hurried out the back door and ran across the junior school playground, passing the familiar outdoor, red-brick male latrines. Furtively making our way out the back entrance onto Chester Road, we turned north towards the park, nervously looking across the street at Mr. Brassington's house for any sign of movement. On the way passing the one location where we ran the risk of being seen by anyone coming out of The Orphanage grounds. The main gates in front of the Governor's house led to the administrative offices and church but fortunately both buildings were closed on Saturdays. None-the-less, keeping a very watchful eye on the windows of the Governors residence as we approached, we carefully moved into the shadows of squared, roadside privet hedges, hoping to escape detection.

On the opposite side of Chester Road, standing in lush gardens was the familiar Nursery School, which had been my home for a few months as a child many years earlier. The old familiar Victorian style building was still being used for newly arrived infants. More recently, however, as a young Boy Scout together with a few young companions, we had camped in the long tree-shaded meadows at the rear for a rare unaccustomed enjoyable weekend. Now and then, from our hidden location, we spotted staff entering and returning up the short driveway through the portal entrance visible from the road, causing a hasty return to the opposite pavement, alongside the farm field, to avoid being seen. Eventually, casually sauntering through the impressive gated entrance to the park, temporally pausing at one of the pump-handled water fountains to drink, we filled our little metal flasks with cold, refreshing water.

Dawdling slowly along the black-topped driveway past the lake, crossing over the tall grass verges, we entered onto the broad naturally festooned pathways winding through the beckoning forest. The damp scent of rotting leaves and pine needles was overwhelming and for a while we ran excitedly kicking over the leaves, gathering fallen edible brown chestnuts, stuffing them into bulging trouser pockets. Later as the sun slanted through the tall branches of trees, we found the hidden place and crawled inside to sit back against the thick roots to discuss our next move. Neither of us really knew what the plan was, or where we were eventually going but at that moment it didn't really matter. We were free and could go and do whatever we wanted until the next day, considered soon enough to make any major decisions.

Supper consisted of munching the girl-friend's school-baked pastry and biscuit, with the occasional crunchy chestnut, washed down with cool fresh fountain water. Afterwards for a short while we talked while preparing the den for the night, covering the soft, moss covered earth with the square groundsheet and positioning the back-packs at one end for a pillow. At dusk, settling down fully clothed, we took the precaution to cover ourselves with overcoats for extra warmth. Mistakenly my little, ill-fitting, black lace-up boots were left on, proving to be very painful later. The hand-me-down boots had always been a little tight but during the night my feet began to swell and the pain became excruciating, causing me to desperately tear at the laces to remove them. It was a lesson well learned for the future.

As long shadows disappeared and the sky darkened unfamiliar noises were heard, rustlings, scampering, squeaks, shrill cries and hoots from above as the wind whistled eerily in the trees and little objects fell noisily to the ground. A totally different sound to the soft autumn breezes we had become accustomed to hearing during the day. Then it began to drizzle, slowly at first dropping through the leafy branches in large plops, then gradually increasing in regularity until becoming a constant downpour. Hastily drawing the ground sheet over our heads we crouched beneath it for a long time, huddling close together, until the rain finally slowed and we lay back to try and sleep. It was difficult with the multiple noises of the night and as the temperature dropped only brief periods of rest were snatched, until daylight finally arrived and the two of us thankfully crawled out stiff and shivering in the early morning mist, to face our first full day of freedom.

There was a great deal of early activity in the surrounding woods, birds chattering in the branches and on the ground, red squirrels flicked bushy tails, frantically gathering acorns and brown-skinned chestnuts. We both hurriedly walked off a short distance from the den to choose a private spot to relieve ourselves, before returning to squat in the hideout. The thought came to mind "At least I won't have to clean the lavatory today or empty the pot!" After consuming the remaining pastries for breakfast then tying on our boots, knapsacks were rolled into the ground sheet and the large wad pushed into a deep corner beneath the roots. After covering the entrance again with a thick bundle of evergreen branches, we strode off back along the blue-bell-bedecked path, leading out of the woods into the open parkland.

At such an early hour there were no visitors so upon arriving at the shallow lake, spotted with open water lily pads, we removed boots and socks to paddle around on the sandy bottom. The cold water eased aching feet, while simultaneously cupping palms to splash over our faces. Beyond the lake, set back from the road, was the derelict, rusting barbed wire encampment, used earlier during the war for Italian or Polish refugees, now abandoned and silent. High-wired gates still padlocked securely, prevented any access to the metal roofed Nissen Huts lined up inside. Once built to keep prisoners in the barbed wire fence now kept us out. I recalled previously passing long hours from opposite sides of the fence, listening to stories of foreign lands and families described in broken English. All seemed peaceful, even the American servicemen were gone whom we had earlier scrounged from, and who had driven the massive iron, rumbling tanks, almost destroying the beautiful gorse-covered hills.

Unknown to us at the time, earlier in the summer, a huge Normandy counter-invasion had begun in Europe. The countryside in the park was now unusually quiet and empty, left to nature, the original animal inhabitants and a few local residents. Both the unfortunate hemmed-in inmates and the free-and-easy American soldiers had always been kind to us "urchins," handing out sweets, food and even cash at various prearranged opportunistic moments. Unfortunately for the two of us at this time, it was no longer to be.

A few early risers walked along the driveway while a group of cross-country runners in shorts and singlet's jogged up the deep rutted slopes, previously torn apart by the earth-grabbing iron tracks of the Allied tanks. Here and there a lone sprig of wild gorse with tiny yellow flowers bravely reached for the sun, from between deep gouges in the once rich soil. The stark nakedness of a previously multi-blossomed rolling hillside was made even more bizarre, by the occasional leafless tree stripped of bark, standing like a tall scaffold reaching upwards in desperation to the heavens. It was no longer a "green and pleasant land," but brown, barren and ugly. I have often wondered since if it was ever finally restored to its original beauty after "Victory in Europe" Day?

Thirsts were easily quenched again from one of the water fountains located throughout the park, but food became a concern very quickly. We had hoped to cadge money from the "Yanks" or food from the refugees, but both those sources were now gone and the average local park visitor was not about to give anything to a couple of scruffy-looking urchins like us. What little coinage shared between us could not have bought very much, even if there were any shops close by, but the nearest one lay behind almost two miles away, close to The Orphanage, where certainly we had no intention of returning.

Later in the day we finished the remainder of the broken biscuits and nuts, satisfying our immediate needs, but towards the second evening upon returning to the den, pangs of hunger returned. As the sun slowly diminished over the horizon it started to drizzle again, dripping through the green, natural canopy high above us, as we huddled beneath the stiff canvas. Gradually temperatures dropped and by dusk we were both shivering uncontrollably. Even with extra clothing the lack of warm food and increasing dampness began to have an affect. It was miserable and even the thought of a customary lukewarm, unpalatable mug of cocoa and lonely iron bed, now caused me to doubt the recent hastily contrived decision.

After what seemed like hours of stiff, cramped sleeplessness I felt my friend move.

"Are you awake?" I enquired in a whisper.

"Yes, it's too cold!" He stammered, adding. "I'm hungry, maybe we should go back?"

Considering his suggestion briefly I ventured an idea; "We could go and find something to eat and perhaps somewhere warmer to sleep?"

"Where can we get food this time of night?" He questioned.

After further pondering I suggested that if we returned to the house and raided the pantry, often done before, we might then perhaps find a door open in one of the many outbuildings on the grounds to hide for the night, another familiar practice. Silent for a while he contemplated my suggestion then suddenly sat upright. "Come on then let's go!"

Grabbing our packs and cramming everything in, we crawled out of the rapidly soaking den to hurry nervously along the now eerily creepy pathway, beneath dark whispering branches, towards the entrance. The trek back from the park along the edge of the main road to the home seemed endless in the half-moon-light, feeling so tired in the grey swirling mist the distance seemed twice as long and very few vehicles passed. As each car's hooded headlights approached we jumped back into the shadows, close to the tall privet hedges, crouching down to avoid being seen. Eventually, mournfully dragging ourselves through the back entrance, close to the familiar red brick Brampton Hall, we crossed the playground into the comparative shelter of the boys' toilet block.

For a short while, resting despondently sitting on toilets in one of the smelly cubicles, we contemplated our next move. Outside it was pitch black and no lights showed in any of the nearby houses. Vaguely I thought about all the other boys laying warm beneath threadbare blankets and thin patterned covers, completely oblivious to our chilly predicament. By now, tiredness and hunger pangs were almost unbearable, but sitting shivering on the icy-cold toilet seats we eventually worked out a desperate strategy to alleviate the problem.

Leaving backpacks behind we stealthily made our way towards Meriden House, carefully staying on one side where the pantry was located. Knowing the back door to the house was always kept locked and bolted all night, I had no intention of trying to break in there. The pantry, however, had a small fanlight window situated just above our heads which opened outwards.

An adjustable bar containing a series of holes, fitted over a little raised stud, made it possible to adjust the angle of the opening. Being much shorter and thinner than my friend I volunteered to try and squeeze through the opening and, with the help of a leg-up, managed to reach the window, release the bar and pry it open to its fullest extent.

By pulling myself up and digging the toes of my boots into the brick pointing, gradually I squeezed my head and shoulders through the narrow gap. Then, as my eyes became accustomed to the dark, just below the window I could see a flat, marble stone shelf with a number of squat glass jars stacked in rows. Lowering myself slowly through the opening, sitting astride the window ledge, I managed to reach the jars and carefully slide them to one side. This cleared a space to stretch down and bear weight on my hands, making it possible to finally stand on the shelf and eventually jump down onto the tiled floor to look around.

There was not much to see in the dim light except a couple of hemp potato sacks on the tiled floor and what appeared to be large tins or jars on a higher shelf. Opening the hooked latch of a mesh-fronted cupboard revealed a metal bin, containing some loaves and a couple of sticky buns in a brown bag. Taking the loaf and bag to the window and kneeling on the shelf I carefully dropped them outside, calling softly "Catch these!" without actually seeing if indeed they were caught.

Stepping back down again to investigate further, realizing any loud noise could have awakened someone, I was careful not to move things around or open other closed cupboards. Having to be so cautious made it more difficult to determine whether there were other edible goodies stored within sight, or reach that could be so easily retrieved.

Not feeling anxious to overstay, or run the risk of being caught inside the narrow room, I finally climbed back up and poked my head out of the little vent window.

"Not much else I can see!" I declared.

"All right you'd better come out," was the whispered reply.

Before attempting to exit, hurriedly grabbing one of the large glass jars from the cold stone slab, I reached down carefully to lower it into cupped waiting hands, with no idea of what the contents actually were but guessing they were probably edible. At that point getting back out-side proved a little more difficult than anticipated.

Jumping up from the shelf, pushing my head and shoulders with some difficulty through the tiny space and wiggling until my stomach lay across the ledge, I stretched down to grab my friend's hand, sud-denly realizing that something low down was being held fast.

The metal stud used to keep the window open had caught in the buttoned fly of my short trousers, leaving me literally dangling by the groin, a very precarious position to be in and one which threatened my future masculinity! However, with great difficulty, by sucking in my stomach and using one hand I was able to extricate myself. Although in the process losing one of the gun-metal buttons, which under the extreme pressure snapped off, pinging back into the room, ricochet-ing loudly between the rows of glass jars. For what seemed an endless moment I fearfully held my breath listening, until finally sliding down to the ground and carefully stretching upwards to close the window, remembering to push the locking bar back inside.

Clutching the swag in waist-scooped pullovers we ran breathlessly back to the toilet block and squatted gasping, the sheer tension and excitement of the escapade having suddenly increased our breath-ing and heart rates. Checking the contents of the jar by match-light, we discovered it contained plump, yellow plums or damsons in rich, sweet syrup. Using a valued Boy Scout penknife to pry the lid open we swigged down the sugary liquid, sucking at the juicy fruit, skillfully flicking the slippery stones into the open urinals from between thumb and forefinger. While sharing the sugary buns and hurriedly gobbling up sticky mouthfuls, the thought occurred to us that maybe for once we had denied the Sisters something that, under normal conditions, would be theirs alone. It was only on very rare occasions we would ever have been offered such delicacies. Following the brief midnight feast we realized how late it was, as cold and fatigue began to overwhelm us, so depositing the brown bag into the back-pack we set out to find more comfortable shelter for the remainder of the night.

Across the football fields at the rear of the houses, a raised wooden pavilion built for storing soccer and cricket equipment, also contained a gang-mower and other tools used to maintain the playing fields. A low wooden veranda extended the length of the building with a waist high balustrade in front, built to protect the seating and viewing area, normally reserved for spectators and waiting players. Fortunately the door was not padlocked but upon entering the dark interior I tripped over a roll of goalpost netting and a thick canvas, normally used to cover the cricket pitches when it rained. The rolls formed a soft, sofa-like, flat shape making an ideal place to lie, so wrapping ourselves in overcoats once again we snuggled down, utterly exhausted, to rest. During the remaining night-time I frequently awoke, feeling uncomfortable and cold, snatching only brief periods of sleep between natures outside noisy occurrences. At first light, rising with stiff aching joints, I clambered up to look out of the dingy, web-covered windowpane at the playing fields shrouded in a low hovering morning mist. Johnnie stirred, mumbling incoherently as he stood shivering beside me at the window.

"What day is it?" he questioned, between chattering teeth.

"Monday," I replied. "We should be at school today."

Later, as if to prove my words, a group of boys carrying book bags passed a short distance away on the path leading to the back gate, obviously heading towards Jockey Road, the main route to Boldmere Secondary Modern School. Hastily ducking below the window as they passed, peering through a broken corner of the dirty pane, we saw yet another group walking by without even glancing our way.

Eventually, concluding everyone had left, for breakfast we ate a hunk of now stale brown bread with the remaining bottled plums and juice. Once the sun had burnt off the early morning mist we ventured carefully outside, knowing our sojourn in the ramshackle pavilion was ended, leaving us free to do as we pleased for the rest of the day, or so we thought!

Behind the perimeter fence at the rear of The Orphanage grounds, neat gardens of private homes were situated on quiet streets, where frequently we were taken for Sunday afternoon walks. Sutton Park was often the Sisters' first choice but alternatively on cooler days, a stroll around the "posh" detached houses or bungalows was closer and took less time before tea. The Sisters always admired the well-manicured homes and well-kept flower gardens, especially Sister Eva who delighted in describing to us the many different floral varieties at every opportunity. Many of the homes had low concrete walls along the fronting pavements, dividing narrow red brick pathways leading to glass-framed porch entrances. A few houses boasted wider driveways to garages, owned only by wealthier families who could afford a motorcar. For others less fortunate public transport was the main means of getting to the workplace. Single-decker "Midland Red" busses covered routes to nearby towns, although most residents walked the short distances to local vendors for their daily shopping needs.

Exiting the single back gate and following the road leading to the school, we eventually turned into a cul-de-sac, walking along the narrow pavement peering at each house in turn, looking carefully into the porches to see whether the milkman or baker had visited. Well practiced, over the years, in the art of thieving from front door ledges, where tradesmen frequently left their wares, we were hoping to find another means of augmenting our meager food supply. On this particular day however deliveries had already been made and there was nothing to be acquired, probably because this particular day was not scheduled for "rounds," so our source of free sustenance was unfortunately, for the time being at least, denied.

An elderly lady weeding her garden early looked up as we passed and smiled, completely oblivious to our evil but necessary intentions. It was a friendly benevolent smile, unlike the grim scowls we had grown accustomed to. I almost felt compelled to stop and make a personal monetary request but continued past without acknowledgement, except to smile back. I was to recall her kind, motherly face for years afterwards, somehow at that moment finding it easy to recognize a lady who had obviously once raised a family and understood childhood needs and aspirations.

The remainder of the day became a blur, walking aimlessly for hours ending up in the High Street of Sutton Coldfield, the closest town, where open-fronted shops and the only local cinema were located. In the past on rare occasions we had been taken there to "window shop," or once, having been very well behaved, I was actually included in a group visit to a Saturday morning matinee.

Two films were generally shown, usually a Western or perhaps a Science Fiction with an added cartoon. Favorites were Buck Rogers, Tom Mix, and Hop-a-Long Cassidy plus of course the early Disney characters, Mickey, Donald and Goofy. Snow White and the Seven Dwarfs became the most popular children's movie at the time, along with classic war films and the news from the war front. Everyone knew the words to the cartoon's songs, "Hi Ho, Hi Ho, It's off to work we go," "I'm Wishing," etc.

Walking around the various shops we could only look, or drool, at the aromatic displays in the baker's window, or the fresh scent of succulent fruit. Without any money there was no hope of sampling any, even though we tried looking appealingly through the display windows at the lone proprietor, sporting his starched white apron.

By late afternoon, dragging our feet along the pavement, tired and hungry, we ultimately decided running away was not really a good idea. Reluctantly we turned and headed back toward The Orphanage, on the way catching up with a group of boys returning from their full day at school, who were surprised to see us as we joined them to reenter the back gate. Every step taken across the playing-fields towards the houses was made with sheer fear and trepidation, imagining the inevitable dire consequences.

Anticipating the reception we were likely to get from Nellie Hunter we sidled in through the back door behind the other boys, to hide our knapsacks on one of the low shelves in the boot room. Plucking up courage, walking boldly forward down the long hallway leading to the sitting room, I knocked nervously on the door.

"Come in!" commanded the easily recognized, dreaded voice.

Cautiously turning the brass knob I poked my head slowly around the edge of the door. Sister Nellie looked up from darning a sock, pulled tightly over a mushroom shaped wooden peg in her hand, quizzically staring at me over her rimless glasses as if trying to recognize my grubby, disheveled form.

"Oh? So you're back, you horrible little boy. Where is the other monster?"

My friend squeezed slowly sideways past me into the room.

"Here Sister"! He exclaimed hesitantly. For a moment there was silence as she surveyed us both, looking us up and down in obvious disgust. Then finally she commanded:

"Get to the bathroom! You're both filthy!"

Obediently we turned and scuttled frantically back down the hallway to the bathroom, feeling thankful that no physical punishment was scheduled to be doled out, at least not immediately.

"Maybe we are too old or too big for her to punish?" I vaguely wondered.

Following us into the cold, white-tiled room, Sister Nellie ordered us to remove our clothes and climb into the large enameled bathtub. The water, warm for once, felt good and we languished, bathing for a while, until as we were drying ourselves, Sister returned, throwing our nightshirts at us and directing we dress and follow her. Ushering us up two flights of stairs to the top landing we were pushed into the familiar, uninviting Isolation Room and the door locked behind us.

Once again I lay uncomfortably on the thin mattress, atop the iron-framed bunk-bed staring at the cracked ceiling, except this time at least there was somebody else to talk to. "We will see what Mr. Roycroft has to say about this tomorrow," was her parting comment. Lying beneath the thin single blanket worrying about the next day, the previous two sleepless nights caught up with me and I finally fell sound asleep.

Early next morning we were let out, sent back downstairs and after the usual breakfast of stale bread and lumpy, lukewarm porridge, while preparing for school we learned our fate.

"No school for you two today, Mr. Roycroft wants to see you both!" stated Sister Nellie.

So that was it! We were to meet with the Governor himself not the anticipated Discipline Master. Obviously we had really done it this time and, as feared, were indeed now too grown up for the sister to punish us herself.

After all the other boys had departed for school we were escorted out of the house, around the oval pathway to the imposing front office adjourning the church. At the top of a wide staircase the Head Sister directed us into a large, wood paneled room and ordered us to sit on a planked bench just inside the door. Two young women in pretty floral frocks, seated at separate desks faced us, busily fingering the keys of black upright typewriters, only pausing momentarily as we entered to look enquiringly at Sister Nellie.

"These two boys are here to see Mr. Roycroft," Nellie Hunter announced, as she breathlessly flopped down into a deep, brown leather armchair in the opposite corner. Without giving us a second glance one of the women quietly stood, walked across the lush carpeted floor to a solid wooden door on one side, knocked delicately and entered. The second younger typist looked across at me briefly with a kind of reassuring, yet pitying look, as if knowing what was about to happen. The brief wait seemed endless causing me to fidget, which brought about a quick scowl from Sister, but at that moment the secretary returned and beckoned to my friend sitting alongside. "Mr. Roycroft will see you first," she explained.

Johnnie stood up glancing at me with raised eyebrows, slowly shuffling across the room as the secretary closed the door behind him, before returning to her desk to fidget nervously with a stack of papers while intently gazing down at the typing machine. I vaguely wondered why she appeared so apprehensive, when it was the two of us who were about to be disciplined.

No sound emitted beyond the thick walls and solid paneled door, until a short while later my friend came out and beckoned with his head for me to go in. His face was flushed with tear filled eyes and one hand was clasped inside the other as if holding something tight. I knew it was not a present! Rising slowly under the blank expressionless stare of Nellie Hunter I crossed the carpeted floor and carefully pushed open the door to enter.

"Shut the door!" a deep voice growled.

He was seated in a deep leather chair behind a squat dark wooden desk, facing the door. Above broad padded shoulders, beneath black wavy hair, dark, deep-set eyes stared at me. Large, veined hands lay flat on the desk, with fingers spread outwards across a square pink blotter covered in hieroglyphics and ink stains.

I had met the Governor numerous times before, walking around the grounds, at the annual Christmas Party and of course observing him reading a gospel text in church on Sundays. He always appeared such a kindly man, patting boys gently on the head and asking, "How are you today?" There was only one other occasion before when he had scolded me, during an earlier described summer, when I unfortunately almost collided into him wearing roller skates, while propelling my brother in a wheelchair around the oval path.

At this particular moment however, he did not look kindly upon me as he glared from beneath bushy eyebrows, slowly raising his hands and interlocking the fingers, whilst leaning his elbows on the desk. Standing sheepishly in front I glanced nervously around the room, anywhere but at his angry face, with arms stretched straight down my sides, rubbing damp palms against the rough serge of my short trousers.

"You have caused a great deal of trouble and concern, young man!" he stated, as our eyes met. "We must learn that running away will not be tolerated!" I vaguely wondered who the "we" were, or if indeed he also needed to learn the lesson.

Still speaking he rose and slowly strode over to an open-topped, leather-bound, box-stand in one corner and removed a long, thin, bamboo cane from among a variety of walking sticks and umbrellas. Stepping towards me he swished the cane through the air a couple of times as if testing the flexibility, causing me to blink and wince at each sound. Carefully positioning the cane below my wrist raising my arm, he commanded me to stretch out my hand. From between clenched teeth he murmured; "As the instigator, you will receive double punishment!" I vaguely wondered what an instigator was as the cane suddenly swept down, striking my outstretched fingers and cutting into the flesh with agonizing pain. Three times he struck before repeating the process on the other hand, as reddening welts began to swell on the first. Fighting back tears I stared at the wall behind him, refusing to show pain, gritting my teeth as he grasped either side of my chin firmly between thick fingers, slowly turning my head until our eyes met.

"I never want to see you here again, do you understand?"

"Yes Sir!" I mumbled, hardly able to speak but thinking; "Not if I can help it."

Upon leaving the room, the Governor thankfully turned the door handle to let me back into the outer office, where the two young secretaries still stared intently at their typewriters. Without looking back Nellie Hunter led us downstairs, out into the bright sunlight, along the circular footpath to the house. On the way commenting with a tight-lipped smirk that perhaps we should think carefully before running away again. Unknown to me at the time, related later by my sister Pauline who on occasions helped with housework in Meriden, Sister Nellie had commented earlier in a sarcastic tone, "Your brother's gone again!" Of course, I had been known to be absent a few times before, although for much briefer periods.

Adding insult to injury, instead of attending school for the rest of the day we were both kept busy with housework, including scraping and scrubbing the pockmarked red tiled floors in the boot room. The necessary buckets of cold water actually proved a form of relief for blistered palms, which otherwise would probably have gone untreated.

By evening the skin over the welts had shriveled into dead blisters and at mealtime even the usual inedible, over-cooked mish mash served up was scoffed down with relish. Later that particular night, lying awake uncomfortable and lonely in the dark, a vow was silently made that if ever I attempted to run away again most certainly I would never return.

12

Final Escape

The one lesson learned from previous attempts at running away was the importance of prior planning, realizing it was not enough just to take off for a few hours or even a couple of days to live a gypsy type of existence, only to discover that money, food, and somewhere comfortable to sleep were important. Early in 1945 I began seriously to consider how to get away and hopefully return back home, encouraged by the fact that my sisters had already left and my brother and I were permanently separated, made me even more determined to succeed. The plan was discussed with Maurice on different occasions whenever we briefly managed to see each other, although he was never really enthusiastic to accompany me.

Following our earlier dual confrontation with Sister Nellie he was transferred to Seymour House next door, where the head sister in charge was Sister Lillian. During his time there he experienced one particular incident, prompting him to retaliate in self-defense, after being repeatedly cuffed around the head with her hand for some obscure minor offence. Retaliation to such punishment was of course virtually unheard of and following the standard procedure, he was taken to the Governor's office to receive the customary thrashing with a bamboo cane. Fortunately he was not so regularly subjected to the more frequent abuses endured by me at the hands of Holloway, Hunter and Brassington.

My brother was and is by nature a more easy-going person, prone to avoid confrontations unless provoked whereas my reaction, being of a more highly tempered nature, tended to be more violent when confronted, which of course frequently meant more trouble and subsequent punishments. Maurice was assured that if and when I arrived home Mum would learn the truth about how we were treated, feeling certain he would then be sent for. Eventually however, he was transferred to another branch named Harpenden, near London, much closer to home, where he stayed until eventually being released. Having previously been pronounced "The Instigator" and suffering double punishment as a result of my last attempt at running away, I was careful this time not to include any other friends in this latest scheme.

In May of 1945 "Victory in Europe Day" was celebrated and everyone attended a special Sunday service in church, where the former Governor, Mr. Jacka, resplendent in his Royal Air force uniform, conducted the service. As he spoke I couldn't help recalling an incident Pauline had once related, describing how he had deliberately spanked her naked buttocks with his hand as punishment for being "naughty!"

Many street parties were held throughout major cities and the suburbs, but I do not remember any particular celebrations taking place at the home, except for one brief visit from the Lord Mayor of Sutton Coldfield. One memorable day, however, we were taken out to line up along the pavement of Jockey Road and wave little paper "Union Jacks" on a stick, as King George VI and Queen Elizabeth passed by in a huge open topped Rolls-Royce limousine. The chauffeur in his black uniform and shiny peaked hat reminded me so much of my Dad and one earlier happy day, when he had driven the whole family to the coast at Southend-on-Sea, that I hardly noticed the "Royals".

My initial concern at the time was how to raise enough money to pay for bus and train fares, particularly having only a vague idea of how much they may be. However, I knew there was a difference between an adult ticket, a child's and a return ticket, which I had no intention buying, of course. One of my regular sources of income, particularly during the war, came from scrounging or bribing fraternizing American Servicemen, but unfortunately they had long since left the park. War souvenirs, including empty bullet cases and pieces of shrapnel picked up from nearby bomb craters, had also long since been swapped or sold to better off local students.

Attempting to save my three pence a week pocket money at this time was extremely difficult, because not only was it frequently denied for some petty reason, but also on the rare occasions it was received hunger demanded that it be spent on extra food. Many weekly allowances would have been needed to raise sufficient funds to pay the anticipated fares, guesstimated to be at least ten shillings or one hundred and twenty pence, amounting to forty weeks of saving, almost a year, considered far too long to either wait or be able to save the money.

Autumn was football season and many local teams visited at weekends to play matches against the home team. Games were played on The Orphanage pitches by adult teams from outside who did not have their own suitable place to play, so on most Saturdays during the season all soccer fields on the grounds were in use. Some local teams arrived by motor coaches which were parked alongside the gravel road between the back of the houses and the playing fields, while most other players who lived nearby arrived on bicycles, with only a privileged few traveling by car.

In the upper Infant School playground an open-sided, corrugated metal-roofed shed contained a bicycle rack and a small changing room at one end, with wall clothes hooks and low wooden benches where some of the visiting players left their personal property. A few bikes were chained and padlocked but most were stacked side-by-side in the front wheel rack, or leant against one of the walls or wooden supports. For any boy who did not own a bike and to whom it appeared never would, the sleek drop handled speedsters parked in their own backyard frequently proved to be just too much of a temptation.

Consequently most Saturday afternoons, when the whistle sounded the commencement of games, there was a rush to the shed by some

of the older boys, each one making for the brightest and speediest looking machine with the sole intention of trying it out. Once mounted the
upper quadrangle became a virtual cycle track, with young contestants
pedaling furiously around the perimeter or down the narrow pathway
behind the boy's houses, out of sight of the playing fields hidden by
rows of tall poplar trees.

Posted lookouts signaled halftime when all bikes were hurriedly
returned, hopefully to their original places. During the second half the
process was repeated with first half watchers getting their own turn
at the fun. This system was of course flawed, as we discovered, owners eventually became very suspicious about their machines and the
familiar group of "home" boys sitting on the wall looking nonchalant,
particularly when seats or handlebars were raised, lowered or twisted
to suit obviously slighter statures. Other bodily telltale marks included
grazed knees, elbows or black greasy chain smudges on bare calf mus-
cles, meaning discovery was eventually inevitable, which turned out to
be a blessing for me.

At the age of thirteen, not very tall but known to be a little feisty I
commanded certain respect from my peers, so it may have appeared to
visiting team members that amongst at least one particular group of boys
I was the leader. Naturally they approached me to negotiate terms for the
protection of their property and eventually it was agreed, in return for
keeping an eye on their bikes during the game and ensuring they were
not ridden, we would be paid a monetary reward in the amount of half a
crown (thirty pence). Even divided between three or four boys this was a
great deal of money so the offer was readily accepted.

Additionally, for a few weekends, extra personal cash from owners
was earned for cleaning and oiling their bikes, using tools and a little
flat squeeze-pop oilcan kept wrapped in leather saddlebags. In the process I became quite a proficient cycle mechanic, and having to test the
smooth running of each machine after servicing was also able to enjoy a permitted brief excursion now and then. Throughout remaining
Saturdays, before the end of the football season, sufficient money was

saved for anticipated expenses, so detailed planning for the big escape really began in earnest.

Behind houses adjoining the toilet block were several coal or coke bins. Squat, concrete structures with sloping corrugated iron roofs and rectangular wooden lids set on top in the center. In front, low to the ground, each one had a sliding, guillotine-type removable metal hatch, which when lifted made it possible to shovel out fuel. Seldom was the hopper full as each house was rationed according to the number of occupants and frequency of use. Consequently there was always quite a large empty space inside, often used for hide-and-seek, much to the chagrin of the sisters who frequently knew our hiding place, doubtless because of coal-dust-stained clothes and faces.

During my previous brief evacuation to the Morton's in Derbyshire, at the height of the war, a dilapidated canvas-covered suitcase had been loaned for the trip. Upon returning it was placed in the low attic cupboard at the far end of the top landing, where many other similar bags were stored. Realizing something similar was needed to carry at least a change of clothes and personal belongings, the decision was made to "borrow" one for the anticipated lengthy journey.

One Sunday evening, after pretending to be sick following tea, I was sent up to bed while the Sisters and remaining boys departed to attend the evening church service. Evensong was one service always enjoyed because it often included a few favorite hymns, without having to endure the morning's lengthy, boring sermon. However there were more important things to take care of during the time it would have taken to attend that night.

The moment everyone had left the house for church I ran up the stairs along the top landing, to sort through the selection of suitcases and leather valises to find a suitably easy to carry case. Fortunately there were a large number to choose from and eventually I decided on a small lightweight, canvas covered bag that appeared roomy enough to hold my few possessions. Giving little thought as to whom the original owner may have been I carried it back to the bedroom, discovering days later that it actually belonged to Sister Nellie!

The first items packed were my "Sunday best" clothes, hastily removed and neatly folded, together with better fitting shoes and socks. As there was plenty of space left one of the thin red blankets was taken off the bed and laid on top, not wishing to be caught out in the cold at night again as on previous escapades. Hopefully it would be possible to change back into these smarter clothes at some convenient point before arriving back home. Hurrying downstairs out the back door, dragging the case across to the coalbunker, it was hidden in a dark corner away from the front hatch just in case someone had to fetch coke during the evening. It was my intention to leave very early next morning in weekday clothes before anyone else was about, ensuring a head start before my absence was noticed.

Upon returning to the house I fortunately made it upstairs to the bedroom before the others came back from church. Kind Sister Eva actually came to see me to commiserate and after being readily assured that I was feeling better allowed me down, wearing my threadbare dressing gown. In the dining hall the ritual nighttime cocoa was served, proving to be the last mug of the nasty concoction I was ever to consume.

That night, hardly daring to sleep, a myriad of thoughts evolved around my head as bus stops, trains, stations, roads and buildings appeared in an endless panorama, all watched over by the ghostly hovering apparition of Sister Nellie, eventually everything converging into a restless, murky haze.

At first light, slipping out of bed and dressing quickly in normal weekday clothes I exited the room, unnoticed by the other huddled forms. Descending the stairs, pausing only at the cloakroom to grab my ill-fitting serge overcoat from the numbered peg, I quietly slid the bolt on the back door and carefully closed it. Running swiftly across to the coalbunker, lifting the wooden hatch to reach inside for the hidden case and grabbing the handle, I excitedly pulled it out through the little opening, turning startled to look straight into the face of my brother, who had suddenly appeared immediately behind me.

"Hi our kid!" which was his typical greeting.

"What are you doing?" He questioned in the local Midlands dialect.

"I'm going' home, do you want to come?" replying, forgetting how little money I actually had.

"I would but have to deliver the bread" he said, pointing to the little three wheeled baker's cart he was holding. The designated delivery rounds started early every weekday morning, for both bread and milk, to all houses on both sides of The Green oval.

"Want some bread?" He enquired holding out a small brown loaf he knew was liked, but normally only placed on the sisters' table. Not wanting to get him into trouble for being short I refused, assuring him once again, "I will get Mum to send for you!" After a hurried goodbye I reluctantly turned, walking toward the back gate carrying the little case. Passing through the forbidding pillars with the sawn off black metal stumps, I turned to wave at Maurice who stood watching me in almost disbelief, still holding the long handles of the two-wheeled baker's cart. It was destined to be the last time we would see each other for many years.

On the far side of Jockey Road, opposite to where I had so often waited hoping to meet my Mother was the bus-stop for downtown and railway station. It didn't take long to walk the short distance from The Orphanage and soon I was standing outside the imposing Convent entrance nervously waiting for a bus, hoping my absence had gone un-noticed. At any moment fearfully anticipating that Mr. Brassington or Sister Nellie, or both, would come bustling down the Chester Road to drag me complaining, yet forcibly back.

At that moment the welcome "Midland Red" double-decker bus to town arrived and I quickly stepped up onto the rear platform, excited that my journey home had finally begun. Handing the conductor the requested fare I sat back to peer out the window at familiar, recent summer, suburban street scenes.

The City of Birmingham, had not changed much since my previous visit earlier in the year, but in the railway station everything was covered in black grime including the buildings and the arched, metal and glass domed roof. Many of the glass panels were still shattered or cracked between twisted metal frames, obviously damaged by wartime bomb blasts yet to be repaired. It was a vast, noisy area permeated by coal fumes, steam and damp fog, with hundreds of pedestrians scurrying past, separating through variously numbered iron gates leading to platforms, where huge soot-covered trains stood belching soot and hissing steam. In one corner, through dingy glass windows, customers could be seen seated at tables in the "Lyons Corner Tea House." Walking over to the high counter I ordered a cup of tea and a toasted currant bun. After having missed breakfast hunger pangs surfaced and I considered the few pennies' cost well worth it.

Ticket booths were set off to one side in a separate, grey stone building and at each one a man wearing a shiny peaked cap sat behind a little glass screen, issuing tickets for every journey listed outside on the front of a huge display board. I craned my neck upwards to read the black-lettered signs, continually changing, flashing first one name then another, utterly confusing me. Finally giving up I decided to ask the elderly man at the booth, who obviously had been watching me closely.

"Where do you want to go young man?" he asked, looking over his rimless spectacles.

"London," I replied boldly.

"Single or return ticket?" (I certainly don't want to come back) I thought.

"A single child" I ventured knowing it was the cheapest.

Leaning out of his hatch he peered down at me quizzically from top to toe.

"How old are you, boy?"

"Thirteen," I answered rather proudly and truthfully, proving to be a mistake.

"A child's ticket is for twelve and under," he insisted. "You need a single adult ticket!" Glancing at a printed card on the shelf in front of him, he looked down at me again and announced the price of the ticket, adding, "Single to London, stopping at Coventry!"

I cannot remember the exact quoted fare, but at that moment my heart dropped after hastily counting the few remaining coins in my hand, realizing there was not enough money due to having bought the large currant bun. Desperately turning away from the window and morosely sitting down on a nearby wooden bench, I recounted the handful of coins yet again whilst considering my predicament. Realizing I had to save enough to pay for the bus fare from the center of London to Essex, it occurred to me that if I only purchased a ticket to Coventry, the halfway stop, maybe there would be enough left for the final leg.

Hesitantly walking up to one of the other nearby window booths, not wishing to confront the same teller again, I ordered a single to Coventry, reluctantly handing over most of my small change for a little green cardboard ticket, hastily clutched in my hot little hand, feeling quite proud of my ingenuity.

Later, passing through the black wrought iron entranceway to the designated platform, where the spluttering iron monster waited, I stopped briefly to inquire of a passing porter if this was the train to Coventry?

"This is it, sonny, stopping at Coventry then nonstop to Euston Station, London."

Excited but apprehensive, climbing up the high metal steps to pass along the narrow wood paneled corridor, I sat down in the far corner of a smoky, third class compartment close to the thick glass window. Even on tiptoe the high luggage rack was beyond reach but the case fitted easily under the broad cushioned seat, protected by my short legs dangling over the edge. Suddenly a shrill whistle sounded and the train jerked forward, moving slowly at first as the engine loudly belched out puffs of black smoke, gradually getting faster until finally settling into a rhythmic rattling "clickety clack, clickety clack!" "I'm going home, I'm going home," the rhythm blended perfectly with my thoughts as I lay back to doze, completely alone.

"Next stop Coventry!" The conductor's shouting awoke me as he passed by the compartment door in the corridor. Realizing nobody had checked my ticket the thought suddenly occurred to me, "What if I just stay on the train?" having no idea at the time that between Birmingham and Coventry tickets were not checked on the train, but as you exited from the platform. Settling snugly back into my seat as the train slowed, pulling into the station, I vaguely wondered how I could sneak through the platform exit upon arrival in London.

Screeching to a grinding stop the doors on the platform side were noisily flung open by passengers alighting at the famous "Cathedral City," which had suffered so much from the incessant wartime bombing. Approximately half of the planned journey was now covered, but even with misgivings about the remainder, I told myself that every mile traveled was one further away from the horrible place left behind and one closer to home.

Self reflections were suddenly interrupted when the compartment door was once again flung open and a huge, bolster like kit bag thrown inside by a burly uniformed American soldier. Others, similarly loaded, followed him and soon the empty compartment was crammed full of servicemen. Packs were hurriedly unstrapped from around shoulders and tossed up into the overhead rack with sheer abandon, the owners obviously relieved to be rid of the weight. One of the men sat huffily down beside me as I nervously sidled away, huddling a little more into the corner against the window to make room for his bulky frame.

"Hi there young fellow, you all alone?" he drawled lazily.

"Yes," I replied, "I'm going home!"

"Well so are we," he declared, smiling.

The other men nodded approval grinning at me, until soon we were talking about all manner of things as the train once again puffed its way out of the station towards Euston. The servicemen explained how they had all been "over there" in Europe fighting and now, after the German surrender, they were going back to America to see their families. Some showed photos of children about my age who were obviously far better fed and more smartly dressed than my restricted orphaned friends left behind.

The carriage began to quickly fill with tobacco smoke making me cough, as one very large cigar-puffing soldier offered me chocolate and gum, readily accepted and scoffing the bar hungrily, while stuffing the flat packet of gum into a trouser pocket for later.

Outside the misty window scenes flashed by of multiple buildings, trees and green meadows with grazing cows, all distorted by spiraling raindrops and occasional glimpses of the sun. Once again reverie was suddenly shattered as the heavy sliding carriage-door slammed open and an elderly uniformed conductor stood in the entranceway.

"Tickets, gentlemen?" he demanded.

Crouching and shrinking back against the corner of the seat trying not to breathe, I was fortunately half hidden by the bulky khaki-clad conscript sitting beside me. Each soldier in turn produced a military train pass, leaning forward to present them to the conductor in the doorway while I sat perfectly still, desperately hoping not to be seen. Incredulously after peering briefly at the proffered papers the official turned and with a parting "Thank you, gentlemen," moved out into the corridor without even a glance in my direction. To this day I still wonder whether the conductor really did not notice me, or whether he presumed I was a member of another ticket holding family in an adjoining compartment. Fate obviously does have flights of fancy!

Gradually letting my breath out, as the men replaced the passes inside their tunic pockets, I relaxed back once again on the bench-type padded seat. My "buddy," crammed next to me briefly showed me his pass, much larger than the tiny cardboard ticket still firmly grasped in my hand. For some unknown reason, neither he nor any of the other passengers seemed to notice or care that I hadn't produced a ticket, causing me to vaguely wonder whether tickets were only checked on the train, or if indeed they were supposed to be shown upon arrival at Euston. As if to approve of my feeling of relief, if only temporary, the rain stopped and sunlight covered the countryside, enhancing the greenery and highlighting the multiple shades of late summer foliage. The remaining journey became a very enjoyable travelling experience in the company of the friendly "Colonials."

Eventually the engine crawled, clanging up to the buffered barrier with steam hissing from behind huge iron wheels, noisily grinding to a halt as leather hinged doors snapped open and passengers descended, hurrying along the grimy platform towards the framed exits. Slowly, reluctantly following my travel companions to the gateway, almost engulfed by them, I nervously peered between their bulky frames for the ticket collector. To my extreme relief no one was there as I passed through into the dank capital city, carrying the borrowed dilapidated case, wearing my ill fitting serge overcoat, escorted by a virtual color guard of the United States Military.

Leaving the imposing pillared entrance of Euston Station and entering into the bustling streets of the city, thronging with pedestrians and noisy vehicles, a complete kaleidoscope of utter confusion confronted me standing for a brief moment in awe. Having never seen so many people hurrying by, all intent on going somewhere and appearing to know where, I was obviously the exception. Knowing my destination but not knowing how to get there was my own problem.

Suddenly noticing a London Policeman approaching panic surfaced, and as the shiny-buttoned, uniformed figure towered over me I nervously looked down at the polished toes of his large black boots, thinking;

"He knows I've run away, they must have notified the police!"

The mustached face strapped below the tall cone-shaped helmet seemed friendly enough, but as he held out a white-gloved hand and touched me lightly on the head I instinctively cringed, thinking; "This is it, I give up!"

"Have you just arrived young man?" he questioned.

"Yes, officer," I replied, trying to sound calm. "I've come from Birmingham and I'm going home to Romford!" "That was quite a trip, were you evacuated there?" he enquired smiling benevolently, obviously he had seen many young travelers arrive alone at the station since the end of the war.

I was aware of the government's practice of evacuating children to the country during the blitz, because of the brief summer holiday in the Derbyshire Hills with the Morton Family, so innocently I lied;

"Yes, in the country." Then continued on quickly to explain how my most immediate need was to know how to catch the bus to the town of Romford, where my Mother lived.

"Well, that stop is not far from here if you know the shortcuts, but you shouldn't go alone, come on I'll take you." Firmly taking me by the hand he led me away from the wide, hectic thoroughfare into a maze of dark, narrow streets and side alleys, past numerous piles of brick rubble and blackened bombed out shells of houses, until finally emerging into another wide, busy highway where traffic endlessly streamed by. The air was foggy and damp, reeking of cigarette smoke, puffed out by passing pedestrians, mixed with toxic exhausts from numerous vehicles. The aroma of beer and cooking emitted through open doors of pubs, cafes and shops lining the pavement.

"Over there, outside the entrance to the tube station you'll see the bus stop, do you know the number?" the policeman enquired, as he guided me past the center bollard and across the wide road between the constantly flowing traffic. Giving an assurance, feeling relieved that my first introduction to a unique "London Bobby" had ended with a cheery wave I strode off down the pavement.

On the far side, close to the entrance of the "Aldgate East" underground station, the bus-stop sign bearing the number I wanted was easily located, before joining the end of a long queue of people already formed. It was obviously very close to the end of the workday, because quite a few businessmen, or city-types, in long, dark overcoats sporting bowler hats or soft brimmed trilbies, stood in line with others less fashionably dressed, presumably working men in soft flat hats and rain jackets. Ladies wearing multi-colored headscarves tied under their chins carried large shopping bags or clutched purses, with parcels placed at their feet, apparently having spent the day shopping for bargains at well known major city stores.

By the time the bus finally arrived it was overcast, lights from multiple shops and lampposts were reflected in puddles on pavements and roads. There was a sudden surge and bustling as people pushed forward to clamber aboard the low platform at the rear.

For one moment I hardly managed to get on board because of the crush, the uniformed lady conductor leant down to gently haul me up, declaring in a broad cockney accent, "Room for a little-un! 'Ere love, sit 'ere!" Pointing to a corner space just inside the door on the lower deck, where I obediently sat on the high padded seat, my feet dangling over the high front edge, resting on top of the little suitcase.

"Give me your case!" She stated, taking a firm hold of the leather handle and placing it carefully in an angled space beneath the stairs, leading to the upper open deck.

As the bus began to move off the conductress gradually passed down the center calling out, "Fares please!" Each time a ticket was punched a shrill bell rang on the little squat metal machine hanging on her thick leather waist belt, while change was given from a thinner suede leather pouch slung across her shoulder. On her hands she wore dark woolen gloves with the ends missing, exposing bright red fingernails that matched her lipstick, obviously the uncovered fingers made it easier to count the coinage.

Returning along the aisle the conductress paused and winked at me reassuringly, before ascending the winding metal staircase to the upper level, where the well-practiced ritual was repeated. When the louder bus bell rang, signifying a request stop, the conductress descended the steep stairs to help an elderly couple off with their packages. Then, as the bus began moving again, the lady turned back to stand facing me blocking off the other passengers seated opposite.

"So where are you going Sonny Boy?" She questioned, beaming at me.

Looking up appealingly I replied with confidence, "The Crown, London Road, Romford" having memorized the exact bus stop at the top of the road where my Mothers house was located.

"It's just before the Crowlands School," I added fearing she may not know the area. Raising one eyebrow she replied;

"I know where it is dear but I'm afraid you're on the wrong bus, you want the 86A! This is number 86 we only go to Ilford and Hainault along the Eastern Avenue"!

Realizing the mistake for one terrible moment panic set in, but then I remembered the short summer holiday earlier spent with my Aunt and Uncle, who lived alongside the Eastern Avenue.

"That's alright," I stammered, trying to frantically recall the exact location. "Eastern Avenue is fine, just past the roundabout, I'll show you"!

Raising one eyebrow she replied, "Do you have enough for the fare?"

Opening my hand I showed her the few remaining copper coins still clutched tightly between my fingers.

"Dear that isn't enough, will someone be meeting you?" she enquired.

Stammering sheepishly I replied; "No I'm just going home. I've been staying in the country for a while but I can stop at my Aunt's house!"

Her face softened as she responded, "Sent there during the war, I suppose, those damn 'Doodle Bugs?" I nodded in agreement, sensing her sympathy. (Germen V2 rockets were nicknamed "Doodle Bugs")

"Well now just sit tight love and I'll let you know when we're there, don't you worry"! Firmly closing my fingers back over the few coins she returned to the rear platform to let other passengers dismount, as I relaxed back, grateful for the kindnesses shown to me by so many new-found friends. The remaining journey seemed longer than anticipated and occasionally I almost nodded off, attempting to recognize familiar landmarks through the rain-spattered windows. All the way out from the city anxiously peering out, craning my neck, until finally recognizing my Aunt Doris's house, as unfortunately we drove right past it.

Leaping off the high cushioned seat I excitedly shouted to the ticket lady, "There it is!" The bell rang once more as we approached a request sign and the bus slowed to stop a short distance beyond the location. After moving down the aisle to retrieve my battered suitcase from below the staircase, I frantically jumped from the platform onto the pavement, in my haste almost falling across the case.

"You be careful now, love!" was her parting comment as the big red bus slowly pulled away with the kind conductress smiling and waving from the rear. Dragging the case a short distance back along the sidewalk I was soon standing in front of the familiar low walled entranceway, straddled by a green-painted wooden gate. The house was exactly as remembered, with white pebbledash walls and flat metal-framed windows showing delicate lace patterned curtains on either side.

A shaded corner lamp illuminated the interior of the front room, but there was no sign of anyone while lifting up on my toes to press the white doorbell button. After a brief moment Uncle Percy opened the door, peering over his rimmed glasses in disbelief at my disheveled form, wearing short gray serge trousers and knee-length wool socks drooping over little black lace-up boots. In the rush and excitement of the journey I had forgotten to change into my intended "Sunday Best," carefully packed in the suitcase. Meanwhile the ongoing rain had soaked my school pullover causing it to hang morosely around me, presenting altogether quite a pathetic little figure!

"John?" he finally questioned incredulously. "Where on earth have you come from?"

"I've run away!" I replied with a futile attempt at pride, looking up at his sympathetic face. Then with built up emotion and fatigue suddenly overwhelming me I dissolved into tears, just as kindly Aunty Doris appeared in the hallway.

A little while later inside the neat living room, sitting on the broad, deep sofa with a warm drink and a sweet whole wheat biscuit, I blurted out every occurrence of the day and details of numerous other incidents endured over the years. The adults listened intently, Aunt Doris interjecting only with an expressed, "Oh Dear!" or "You poor thing!" Tearfully I explained that the reason for my sudden arrival at their house, instead of going directly home, was primarily because of the confusion with bus numbers, also insufficient money and how their route had been carefully memorized.

At this particular time my Mother did not own a telephone, so after discussing my predicament, interrupted by occasional sidelong glances in my direction, the decision was made to take me home before nightfall in the black, square-topped family motorcar parked in front of the house.

Wrapped in a warm blanket and bundled into the back seat, Aunt Doris sat beside Uncle Percy who took the wheel as we set off down the avenue. Thin beams of light from the mandatory wartime, hooded headlamps pierced ahead into the drizzling smog of the evening, hovering low above the wet, glistening tarmac. The journey to Mother's house wasn't very long and just as my eyelids began to droop we turned onto the London Road, where familiar locations became recognizable.

To our left the red brick "Crown" public house still stood, hardly changed from the previous summer, when I had accompanied my youngest sister to pick up a bottle of pale ale and a five-pack of cigarettes from the off-license for Mum and Uncle Arthur. New laws today forbid the publican from selling alcohol and tobacco to youngsters, but at the time it was common practice for parents to send their children to the local off-license to pick up orders.

Located next to the pub was the square, single story Army Recruiting Center, an imposing brick building where hundreds of young men had signed up for wartime service. Many were never to return from the front lines, including the husband of a friendly neighbor who was one of those conscripted. Without realizing at the time I was later destined to take the Military Oath, from a very persuasive and bodily robust Recruiting Sergeant, in that same building in the very near future.

Across the street stood the sand-colored, stone structure and slated roof bearing the bell tower of the Crowlands Infants School. The original high iron railings had long since been removed and trucked to a munitions factory. Years later they were replaced by other, more modern fencing, surrounding the buildings and tarred playgrounds. Memories came to mind of many happy playful hours spent with young friends in the schoolyard, prior to being whisked north into unknown purgatory. The turning onto Burlington Avenue was a short distance before the school on a corner, with a high corrugated iron fence surrounding a fuel distribution yard, where a long row of tall cab lorry's, attached to massive oval petrol tanks parked. Much later I discovered that "Uncle

Arthur" worked there in an office behind the fence at the rear of the compound, overlooking our back garden, where a wartime air raid shelter still lay half-buried by a huge mound of earth.

During the war when vegetables were in short supply, he apparently often stuck various fresh vegetables on the pointed tops of the metal fence for Mum to collect. Recounting the story, years later, Mum laughingly called it "Cabbage Courting!"

Slowly driving down Burlington Avenue in the half-light, odd numbers could be seen on the front gates of houses to our left. Passing the first six houses, drawing up in front of the seventh, clearly visible tacked on the front door shone a chrome-colored number thirteen. At that precise moment considered to be the luckiest number of my life.

Uncle Percy opened the car door, then taking me by the hand flicked open the little metal latch on the rickety wooden gate, together with my Aunt we walked the last few steps along the uneven flagstone path towards the front door. An ornate crystal chandelier, hanging from the ceiling, illuminated the front living room. Through the lace curtained windows my Mother could be seen sitting in a corner armchair facing the fireplace. Raising the brass handle above the letterbox flap Aunt Doris knocked twice and stepped back as I stood waiting, trembling with excitement and anticipation. There was noticeable movement inside as the oval glass porch light flashed on above us, while Uncle Percy's hand gave my arm a reassuring squeeze.

The door was slowly pulled open by my youngest sister Pauline, who stood for a moment obviously surprised at the sight of the bedraggled, pathetic little figure clutching the well-worn suitcase. Suddenly recognizing me, she excitedly called back over her shoulder announcing, "Mum, it's Uncle Percy and Auntie Doris! They have John with them!" Her high-pitched call prompted a sudden rush from various corners of the house. My sister, Joan, appeared scrambling down the stairs from the upper landing, while Audrey emerged from the kitchen at the end of the hallway, tugging at apron strings around her waist and frantically drying her hands on a tea cloth. Obviously she had been busily engaged in the kitchen, probably washing dishes and utensils after the evening meal.

Behind the girls Mum emerged into the hall from the front living room and following close behind her, the taller frame of "Uncle Arthur," whom I instantly recognized from their joint visit to The Orphanage the previous summer. This time however he was without a jacket and his stiff shirt collar was missing, also his facial expression did not appear very pleased.

My sisters, on the other hand, were obviously excited smothering me in their arms, but the look of disbelief on Mum's face made me hesitate as she leant down to hug me. Aunt Doris held gently onto my hand as we all stepped further into the hallway, as Mum began to question, "What on earth has happened?" My Aunt and Uncle began carefully to explain how I had run away and arrived at their house earlier due to taking the wrong bus. Unfortunately they then proceeded to state in a very firm manner what they personally thought about Maurice and I being left in a "place like that!"

It rapidly became apparent my escapade was the cause of a very tense confrontation that followed, with both men in particular exchanging very loud, abusive comments and almost coming to blows. As the situation developed the girls were sent into the back room and Joan was directed to take me upstairs to prepare a bed in the little box-room, still used as a sewing room, at the front of the house. Fortunately, having been fed earlier, now tired and very apprehensive over the outcome of the developing scary situation, I was ready to go.

On the way upstairs the sound of adults continuing to argue loudly followed us, causing me to vaguely wonder why everyone was so upset, considering I had only run away to come home and taking the wrong bus was all my fault. Much later discovering that differences the situation had created between the two families gave sufficient reason for them not to converse, or meet each other until many years afterwards. My conscience always bothered me for years over that, until eventually later in life, Mum and Auntie Doris finally came together again.

Lying on the little couch, hastily made into a bed in the tiny room, where the ancient Singer-made treadle sewing machine still stood, one couldn't help but overhear the angry raised voices downstairs. Expressions like, "Shameful treatment!" and "He needs a real mother!" drifted up the stairway. The latter bringing a very loud vehement response from "Uncle Arthur," causing me to cower fearfully beneath the bedclothes.

Eventually, after a seemingly endless period of arguing, the front door slammed violently shut as my real Uncle and Aunt left to drive back up the avenue towards London Road. Standing on tiptoe at the end of the bed, watching through the half open skylight window, they departed, finally disappearing into the darkening mist.

It was to be the last I ever saw of Uncle Percy, who passed away shortly afterwards, and many years before being allowed to visit Aunt Doris again. In the brief period of silence that followed I lay feeling guilty, for causing so much trouble between the people who meant so much to me, wondering why my mother was so angry towards her sister for bringing me home. My immediate concern, of course, was whether I would be allowed to stay home or be sent back to face the wrath of Sister Nellie next morning?

Shortly, whilst contemplating my fate, Mum came to tuck me in for the first time in a decade, whispering an assurance, "Don't worry we will sort everything out in the morning"! Completely exhausted, following the long emotional day, I eventually drifted into a tearful sleep, content in the knowledge that I was finally home, at least for the time being, and not shipped off like numerous other young unfortunates to some foreign land.

Postscript

Whatever the outcome of the argument the night of my unexpected arrival on the doorstep, it apparently convinced Mum and "Uncle Arthur" to announce shortly afterwards that I would be staying home, "at least for a while!" leaving me just a little worried. Ironically we later received a letter from the Home with a check to "cover the sum due" for the hours spent potato picking during the previous summer. Up until that time I never knew we were supposed to be paid for our "forced labor". Most certainly none of the boys had ever received payment in hand at any time, so we could only wonder where all that money actually went! The letter also contained a request for the return of the little battered suitcase belonging to Sister Nellie and the threadbare red blanket taken from my bed. Neither was ever sent back and the squat canvas-covered case served a very useful purpose for many years to come.

For a few months I languished in familiar surroundings so long looked forward to. During that time attendance at the local Whalebone Lane Secondary Modern School was a pleasant experience, making many friends and being taught by one very sympathetic English Teacher who gave me great encouragement. Mum acquired a second-hand bicycle for me to cycle the few miles to school every day, which coincidentally led back up London Road halfway towards Uncle Percy and Auntie Doris' house. Although it crossed my mind a number of times they were never visited, being fearful of parental reproach. The bike also proved useful for cycling errands to the local haberdashery to fetch cottons and cloth for Mum's continuing neighborhood clothing alterations.

More money than ever previously seen was also earned by first delivering the local newspaper and later accompanying Jack the milkman on his horse drawn milk float, placing milk bottles on doorsteps throughout local suburban streets. It was reminiscent of earlier times stealing milk from similar locations in Warwickshire. Jack had been demobilized from the Army after serving in North Africa and he soon became my closest confidant during the brief period spent at home.

Realization slowly dawned that I was not to be the center of attention, particularly with Mum, to whom I had always felt so very close. As the eldest boy in the family it was my childish belief I would eventually become the person responsible for protecting her.

After only a few weeks however, I soon discovered that "Uncle" Arthur had in fact replaced my real Father and was fulfilling the role vacated by him. This realization came as a shock and resulted in numerous confrontations, due to my feelings of resentment towards him and frustration at Mum's apparent lack of understanding. Mistakenly my feelings were often expressed to both adults rather forcefully and one particular teenage tantrum brought a swift physical and verbal response from Arthur, who knocked me to the hall floor by a sudden swift head blow, accompanied by a remonstrating command to "show some respect"!

The force of his anger caused a hasty re-consideration of my position and taught me that, although at the time Arthur was not yet married to my Mother, he was indeed the head provider of the family. A form of resentment continued between us however, until finally a solution was arrived at following a discussion with a real relative, Uncle

Sidney, who was also an 'ex-serviceman'. For a time, apart from an occasional confrontation with "Uncle Arthur," life was great, in particular the weekly shopping trip with Mum to the downtown Street Market. Every day out with her presented a unique opportunity to see and mix with an unaccustomed diverse group of local residents and enjoy private moments feeling needed. One of the highlights of the weekly excursion was visiting the ladies gown salon in the high street, where Mum was the alteration seamstress. The smartly dressed sales ladies always welcomed our arrival, smothering me with hugs and plying me with sweet biscuits while Mum attended her customers.

The following year, in the autumn of 1946, after yet another family discussion, I was taken to the familiar Army Recruiting Center building located on London Road. "It will be the making of him!" was the declared expression. So once again my destiny was to leave home feeling unwanted. In 1946 boys were still enlisted at the age of fourteen for "Boy Service," (similar to three years as a cadet at a Military Academy.) Military training and education were given until the age of seventeen and a half, when one was considered a man and accepted into the regular army for a specified period of nine years plus three years on reserve.

On November the fourth 1946, at the recorded height of only 4'6" and weighing only seventy-nine pounds, I was enrolled into "Her Majesty's Service" at the age of fourteen and a half. The recruiting sergeant remarked that I was the youngest recruit he had ever "sworn in" and of the thirty-two other boys who had signed up that day from around London, I was undoubtedly the smallest.

Mum and my Auntie Barbara accompanied me on the bus and tube train to the Mill Hill Army Depot in N.W. London, headquarters of the Middlesex Regiment, which was to be my base for the next twelve years. During the first two months minus a proper uniform, except for baggy rolled up fatigues, until the quartermaster eventually proudly produced my fitted "dress" uniform, tailor-made especially for me! Over the next decade, army life both at home and abroad actually proved to be infinitely more rewarding and enjoyable than the previous sad years spent in the care of the mean Methodist Sisters at the "Princess Alice School."

Shortly after my juvenile escape and unannounced arrival home, my brother, Maurice, was moved from Birmingham and transferred to a hostel for "troublesome" teenage boys located in Highbury, near London. He attended a school in Finsbury Park for a short period, where he found local boys difficult to get along with, particularly when the "Londoners" made fun of his Birmingham accent. Eventually the Sister in charge of the hostel discovered he was constantly playing truant, so he was sent to the main Harpenden Branch, which to this day is still the headquarters of the National Children's Homes. Maurice stayed there until also joining the Army in 1949 at the age of fifteen, consequently we saw very little of each other again until final demobilization years later. We both eventually immigrated to North America where we meet occasionally and reminisce with surviving family members, including my youngest sister Pauline, who resides in Canada and with whom we both shared so many unforgettable experiences decades earlier.

John Anthony Davies. 2015.

This Life

What good is life if content to sit?
We never make the most of it
But stand and stare up to the sky
And dream while life goes rushing by.

What good is time when all we do
Is waste it without meaning to
What good is there in looking back?
Or saying, I wish I'd thought of that"

What good is it if on our way?
We fail to make somebody's day
Or listen to a point of view
And make a heartfelt wish come true.

What good is life, what good are we?
Who cannot leave a legacy?
When a life fully lived, a job well done
Perhaps may help a less fortunate one.
John A Davies. Copyright 1980

CPSIA information can be obtained
at www.ICGtesting.com
Printed in the USA
FFHW012324230719
53838794-59529FF